GETTING
DIGITAL
DONE

mod
op

GETTING

AN EXECUTIVE GUIDE TO GROWTH
AND TRANSFORMATION

DIGITAL

ERIC J. BERTRAND

LEN GILBERT

JONATHAN MURRAY

DONE

Advantage | Books

Published by Advantage Books, Charleston, South Carolina.
An imprint of Advantage Media.

ADVANTAGE is a registered trademark, and the Advantage colophon is a trademark of Advantage Media Group, Inc.

Printed in the United States of America.

10 9 8 7 6 5 4 3 2 1

ISBN: 978-1-64225-616-1 (Hardcover)
ISBN: 978-1-64225-615-4 (eBook)

Library of Congress Control Number: 2023908259

This publication is designed to provide accurate and authoritative information in regard to the subject matter covered. It is sold with the understanding that the publisher is not engaged in rendering legal, accounting, or other professional services. If legal advice or other expert assistance is required, the services of a competent professional person should be sought.

Advantage Books is an imprint of Advantage Media Group. Advantage Media helps busy entrepreneurs, CEOs, and leaders write and publish a book to grow their business and become the authority in their field. Advantage authors comprise an exclusive community of industry professionals, idea-makers, and thought leaders. For more information go to **advantagemedia.com**.

This book is dedicated to the hardworking team at Mod Op Strategic Consulting and all of the clients, partners, and friends who have made the journey with us.

CONTENTS

INTRODUCTION

We get it; the prospect of change is never easy. We've spent decades driving these changes ourselves and now, sitting with executives who, for years, have done everything right. They've built hugely successful businesses on the backs of top-notch product quality, constant innovation, great channel execution, and a solid brand reputation. They shouldn't need to change yet again, but technological change is a disruptive force that never ceases. For many organizations, keeping pace is a survive-or-die imperative.

The world continues to change. Customer expectations change. Competition changes. Technology change never stops. The opportunity to collect, deploy, and exploit data grows every day, along with its disruptive ability to inform products, pricing, marketing, and virtually every other aspect of a business.

The reality is that what made companies successful in the past is unlikely to remain the key to success in the future. Looking forward, success will be about more than product quality and distribution—it will be about delivering the most effective customer experience, a just-in-time supplies and parts network, data-driven predictive sales and marketing analytics, personalization, and instant agility.

Clients typically don't come to us and demand, "Make us digital!" Instead, they come to us with a business problem: their customers want something that they're not equipped to provide; they don't have the data, or it's not joined up; their infrastructure is running out of capacity; their competition has leapfrogged them;

Digital is a mindset, a way of being and not a piece of equipment.

they see opportunities to innovate but they just don't have the tools, systems, or people they need to execute effectively.

What we realize when we dive in—and what our clients realize as we work with them to find the root of the problem—is that the solutions to most if not all of these issues come back to a fundamental disconnect between the way the world of commerce is evolving today and the legacy systems and processes that so many organizations have become dependent on over decades of investment.

When we talk about becoming digital, people immediately think it's all about technology, but the truth is that technology is likely at the end of a long list of things to be thinking about. Digital is a mindset, a way of being and not a piece of equipment. Being a data-driven, digital business is the way organizations have to operate to succeed today, in an environment where customers and partners (not to mention employees) expect business to be conducted online, frictionless, in a personalized way, and—in virtually every case—through a self-service experience.

Even the most traditional firms are well past the point of communicating with clients and distributors via email, storing their documents in the cloud, transacting via electronic payments, and managing manufacturing, inventory, and logistics with sophisticated resource planning systems. Data and digital connections intermediate all aspects of our business and economy today.

Becoming digital is all about effective exploitation of data—collecting, organizing, and deploying the information required to inform better business strategies, go beyond the baseline commercial requirements, and actually achieve success as a modern organization. An effective data strategy is the foundation of every successful digital business and will determine winners and losers as we stare down the prospect of an entirely new generation of deeply disruptive AI technologies. This book is about how to build a bridge from the past to the future and how to help executives like you envision the kind of change we're actually talking about. Every business has different needs, of course, different strengths and challenges, different markets, and different customers—but what ties it all together is this move toward a more digital mindset, and that's what we set out to illustrate in the chapters to come.

You'll get a sense of what that journey can look like and how digital transformation can make a real difference in what's to come for your organization. Digital growth can mean one of two things: continuing to be successful with your portfolio of products and services but leveling up your interactions with your customers and prospects or creating new data-informed products for your market, understanding what the people in your market need, and taking on the challenge of adopting new AI technologies to meet these evolving desires.

This book is about doing both of those things, and doing them successfully. It's about modernizing business models and developing a real understanding of where your market is moving in the future. Yes, it will likely be enabled by technology in the end, but that's where we finish, not where we start. It's a business conversation, not a technical one. And, ultimately, it's about people—how to serve them, how to help them, how to change for them and with them.

We hope you get something from the pages ahead and that the story helps you better understand the digital direction where the world is heading and how you can be part of that journey.

Good luck, and enjoy the book.

CHAPTER 1

Why Becoming Digital Matters

In this chapter, we are introduced to Sandra, the CEO of Pelican Rental, a global construction rental company, and Mark, a consultant from Mod Op Strategic Consulting. Sandra agrees to meet with Mark after her SVP of operations comes back from a conference recommending Mod Op Strategic Consulting's team. Pelican has been struggling with its digital capabilities and projects, and with the blessing of the executive team and board, Sandra is open to listening to what Mark and his team have to offer.

"I really appreciate you meeting with me and answering some of my questions before we pull the trigger," I said.

"I'm glad to do it," replied Mark.

"My operations guys came back from their conference and were on fire. They talked about what you had said during your presentations and insisted we look into Mod Op Strategic Consulting. I was particularly interested in how you help companies like ours with their digital transformation.

"Do you create software for companies and help with implementing new tech, including AI? I feel we are woefully behind. I keep hearing about artificial intelligence but don't have any idea whether or how it's relevant to my business."

"While we can help with getting the right tech and software in place, and we can absolutely help you take advantage of the huge benefits of AI, that is just a small part of what we do. We provide consulting services to help you become a digital company."

"I have to be honest. We have hired consulting firms in the past, and it has cost us a lot of money. While some of the things they said were helpful, I am not sure we got our return on investment."

"I can appreciate that. But we work in phases. We don't just make a bunch of recommendations and wish you luck. We work closely in developing the vision and the strategies for achieving that plan, and we offer support in executing that plan, including how to effectively communicate and market your new capabilities to your customers. In addition, we make changes to the plan that align with your needs and, in the long run, will save you money, while at the same time helping you grow a data-driven company."

"I'm glad you said that. I feel we need a new approach. We have been focused on new software solutions for our customers, but we aren't getting the response we have wanted, and the software isn't keeping up with demand. We are falling behind our competitors in a market we have dominated for a couple of decades."

"I do believe we can help you with that. You have mentioned software a couple of times, so I wanted to be clear about what we offer. There is a difference between technology and becoming a data-enabled, digital company. While technology is part of the solution, we help your company become digital throughout your entire enterprise and link data in ways that everyone can access and use. The goal is to help your departments become connected to one another and your clients in real time."

"I hate to admit it, but we still accept fax orders," I chuckled.

"Like I said, we don't just focus on outdated technology. My question: How does your current system of taking orders work for you?"

"It's slow and archaic. People don't like not being able to just order equipment and track it online."

"You have captured what becoming a digital company is and what the expectations are now. I would guess that your competitors, especially the start-ups, are already ahead of you because they are built digitally native. That doesn't mean you can't catch up. After all, you have something new companies don't have—expertise, a loyal base of customers, and a strong reputation. Unfortunately, those alone won't help you keep up with the demand for digital."

Many people make the mistake of thinking that being a digital company means that they have new software and technology. Ask a dozen consultants what the term "digital transformation" means and you'll likely get a dozen different answers. The term has become so overused and lacking in definition that it has become meaningless. This lack of clarity is problematic for senior executives charged with leading their organizations through increasingly challenging times.

There's no escape from the fact that the world in which we live and operate today is digital. Transformed or not, all organizations operate in an economy where meaningful transactions and interactions with customers and stakeholders are mediated in the digital realm, and data fuels all of these transactions. The critical question for executives is not whether they can successfully drive a digital transformation but whether they can build a modern operating strategy and model that can thrive in a digital world. Today, of course, that also means incorporating the power of artificial intelligence and deploying these techniques effectively across the organization, including, most critically, in sales and marketing. Even more importantly, can they make these changes in a high-velocity manner to keep up with their competition?

Successful organizations that thrive in a digital world exhibit five key attributes:

- They have empowered cultures where decision-making is pushed outward from the executive team.
- They use data and sophisticated analytics—often in real time—as a foundation for organizational decision-making.
- Automation is deployed as widely as possible to maximize speed and efficiency.
- Service and product design is driven by experimental methods that use users' data to iteratively maximize value.
- Technology decisions are strategic decisions, and resulting technology choices form the foundational platform upon which value-creating products and services will be built.

"I want to thank you for filling out the Mod Op Strategic Consulting Digital Maturity Evaluation. This helps us to determine where on the spectrum of being digital your company lands."

Take the Digital Maturity Evaluation (DME) to determine your digital capabilities at **https://da.dprism.com/**.

"We looked at the results of that, and it was an eye-opener, for sure. The decision to set up a meeting with you was an easy one after that. It looks like we have room for improvement."

"Most companies that have been around a while find there is a gap between their current state and the most modern best practices. It is not an easy thing to recognize that your company needs changes to compete. Some companies dig in their heels and say that they are doing just fine, and that they are still seeing growth. By the time they realize that they have fallen behind, the gaps have become even larger. I applaud you for your foresight and willingness to talk about what we can do for you."

"Some people on the leadership team weren't as convinced. They are allergic to consulting companies based on their past experiences. We've heard of other companies paying millions to groups of consultants and then kicking themselves because they couldn't get their company to adopt the changes recommended. They were left without any practical way to execute change, so it wasted time and money. But I feel what you are offering will be different, just based on that initial assessment."

"I assure you that we will see you all the way through the process, and we have particular expertise around culture, communications, and effective implementation. You're absolutely right that the recommendations are meaningless if they can't get put into place."

My R&D manager, Chris, was our biggest obstacle. He felt we just needed new software, even though we had been working on a new system for a year with no results. His idea was to throw more money at the problem, but I felt it would be good money chasing bad. I did have my own reservations. Chris had made some valid points, but we had to start somewhere in this new digital landscape we were living in. What I was sure of was that we couldn't do it alone, but I was hoping Mod Op Strategic Consulting was the team to help us.

I could not do the same things that had brought us success in the past and still hope to compete in the future.

Mark had hit on an important point about growth, a point that blinded Chris and some others within our business. Pelican had been successful with steady financial growth for our entire thirty years of existence.

I considered that maybe I had been part of the problem in moving the company into the next stage of growth because I was a founder of the company. I had been with the company from the start and developed a business model that had been working for us. For a long time, I couldn't see—and worse, I refused to see—that I could not do the same things that had brought us success in the past and still hope to compete in the future. Even though our revenue was still growing, I had seen a decrease in new customer acquisitions, and some of our loyal customers in the past year had left to work with our competitors. I could continue to ignore it, or I could look at the issue straight on. I asked one of our longest-standing customers why they were leaving. They told me simply that it was easier to work with another company. I offered them some discounts, but they said the price wasn't the issue; it was the ability to order, track, and do business online, twenty-four-hours a day. It was also being able to contact customer service directly online to resolve issues quickly. Billing and tracking invoices was a breeze. And they felt that the other company's systems were adding value to their business in ways we couldn't even contemplate. That was my wake-up call. Everything my customer had highlighted was a result of work being done in disparate systems with zero traceability at our company.

We had to offer more digital services as a company. I knew it was going to be hard to change, but we needed to adapt soon, or I was afraid we would lose our edge in the market space.

To explain what digital means, it can help to start by imagining the opposite end of the spectrum—what some might call an "analog" organization. Think about catalog companies of the past, mailing out paper magazines to customers every month and requiring them to send back order forms with a check. Everyone got the same catalog, with no customization, and tracking someone's purchase history might be limited to an index card in a file cabinet at the home office.

Contrast this with the power of Amazon—not only to allow endless searching and real-time product updates but to surface the kinds of products they think a particular customer is more likely to buy, and even to change pricing on the fly. Think about their ability to run online ads targeting particular demographics or interest groups and how data can drive decision-making in a way that a catalog company could only dream of. Think about how they can use artificial intelligence to answer a customer's questions without spending on human resources—available 24/7.

And, sure, it would be silly to claim that technology doesn't play any role at all in the difference between these two paradigms. Amazon has an incredible infrastructure—and they need it to execute their digital strategy. But that's the point: the strategy comes first. The technology is merely there to enable it.

"We live in a digital world, and there is no escaping it. Data drives virtually everything we do and experience in our typical day. It transcends everything we do throughout our days. It has become so much a part of our lives that we hardly notice it. It is a seamless part of our reality."

"I couldn't agree more."

"Clients today expect a digital experience with the companies they engage with. As leaders, we know what they expect, but there doesn't seem to be a clear road to becoming digital. We can spend many thousands of dollars on consultants writing great plans for everything our business can be, but what is lacking is a clear road map of how to get there."

"I'm still struggling a bit with what you mean by becoming digital. Does that mean everything we do is with technology?"

"Becoming digital is different from just doing digital things; instead, it is how you act as a company. It's about the organization's culture and how you embrace data-enabled decision-making as a means to accomplish your mission and your objectives as an organization. Modern organizations leverage digital capabilities and data to drive improvements in customer satisfaction, product growth, and profitability through efficiency and margin improvements."

Even when people understand what is meant by digital business, they can fall into the trap of thinking that mere "digitization" of existing products and services is enough. We worked with one professional association that was still sending out paper materials to members for them to renew each year. Members would need to fill out a four-page form and send in their payment by mail. Their initial belief was that "going digital" meant moving the form online—word for word, page for page.

After a very short time, the association started to lose renewals—and the initial temptation was to blame the move to digital. "Members must have liked it better the old way," they worried. But they were missing the point. A true digital process isn't just an analog process put on the internet. You have to rethink from scratch and figure out exactly what customers or members expect in a digital environment, recognizing that we all now get exposed every day to world-class digital experiences. Unsurprisingly, members didn't want to have to fill out a lengthy form in order to renew, and so they stopped midway through. We counseled the organization through a process change: get the payment first, and then make the rest optional. Retention rates went back up, even improving compared to the old way of doing business.

The lesson: Becoming digital is not just a mechanical moving of legacy processes online; the digital world is different, and the bar for customer digital experiences has been reset.

"We have been using computers for years and even had a company build us software for our organization a number of years ago. Though I know it's outdated by now, and we need to have it updated."

"What does the software do?"

"Our website had a way for people to send us emails on our contact page, but they couldn't place orders. We have been trying to add a portal to the website in which they could place orders online, but it has been a mess. First, we tried to do it ourselves, but the IT team was overwhelmed with creating it while they still had to execute their regular duties, and programming wasn't their strong suit. They could do simple things to the website, but nothing at the scale we wanted. Then we hired a company that said they could do it. We paid a lot of money, and we were constantly over budget. We finally had to cancel the project because they gave us nothing that would work. It was a disaster, and we should have just set the money on fire for all the good it did us."

"This is not uncommon for us to hear. We strive to create projects with the right people, resources, and technology. We create smaller components rather than just look at the completion of the entire project six months down the line."

"That's exactly what happened. When we got to the six-month mark and were ready to roll out the software, all we got was another proposal for more money to complete the project. We ended it there, but it left a bad taste in the board's mouth, and my CFO was on my case. If we move forward with working with you, we need a real budget with as few overruns as possible."

"We are very transparent. The great thing about our agile approach is that you and your CFO will know in real time how projects are proceeding. The kind of digital strategy we concentrate on encompasses your investment strategy, growth strategy, revenue strategy, product strategy, and sales and marketing strategy. We don't help create technology companies. We help accelerate traditional businesses to become digital ones. We understand this sort of digital transformation can be daunting, but we have the expertise and experience from working with other companies that have

been in similar situations to the one you are facing. We will be here to answer questions any time you have them, and I will be checking with you at least weekly to let you know the progress and to help problem-solve issues that come up."

"We have looked at companies to help us with completing our customer portal, but we are a little gun-shy. In addition, the other department heads all want things to be added to the project. We have no idea how to prioritize all of their requests and also decide what the budget will be. We can't add everything they want."

"This is true, which is why having a strategy is so important. You may realize that the technology you think you need is not necessary at all. Or you may realize there is a large hole in your customer experience that might be solved by technology that you hadn't considered. We will spend the time necessary to decide what you need, and then we will help you prioritize what you need against the goals you are setting for the business."

There are so many elements of being digital that don't even have anything to do with technology. First, there's the respect for data as a foundational business asset and its integration into everything your business does. Just like the difference between an old catalog company and Amazon: data has the power to inform your products, your pricing, your marketing, and every aspect of your business. Everyone today is talking about AI and how it will transform every aspect of our lives. It may, but AI depends on quality data at its foundation. So getting data right is a foundational requirement. We start every engagement with research—about customers' needs and expectations, how customers interact with your business, their levels of satisfaction, your place in the market, and the gaps you can fill. That validated research provides the data to understand where you are and where you want and need to go.

Second, there's the integration across your business. Traditionally, businesses have often been run as a set of siloed departments with handoffs between them. Successful digital businesses are integrated businesses: Information flows throughout the company so that marketing and design and product management are all seeing the same information in real time and working collaboratively, not just passing along information between them and hoping the big picture ends up making sense.

Third, there's the cultural piece. You have to make sure your business is putting customers' needs and experiences at the center of decision-making, embedded into every part of the product life cycle. And as fast as customer needs can shift, as an organization you need the agility to move just as quickly.

It's only with these elements in place that you can begin to figure out which technology tools can help you execute better. But technology is the last step, never the first.

Even if your products are physical, your business still needs to be digital. In today's world, you simply can't survive and grow without being a digital firm. Customers expect self-service, an online platform, and engagement on their terms. Yes, that can require a lot more thought than just investing in new technology, but in the end it's worth it.

I was feeling a little more relaxed the more I talked to Mark. He was right: we needed a strategy and to sort out the elements that were most important rather than trying to do everything at once.

"Consider a manufacturer like Ford Motor Company. Years ago, their strategy was to acquire raw materials, and they had a plant and equipment that they invested in. They employed people to run the machines, which created the parts of cars that they then put together. The cars were loaded on trucks and sent to dealerships that ordered them to sell. Orders for cars were done by phone or even fax machines. A human would take those orders, send them out, and manage the process manually. Modern automotive manufacturers, including Ford, look very different. All the plants and machinery are digital. The company utilizes data from those machines and other sources, such as customer feedback and demand, in making decisions. Data flows from the machinery, and a management system uses that data to optimize every step of the production process. That data can be reviewed, and parameters can be tweaked digitally rather than with a screwdriver or a wrench."

"I get what you are saying."

"Becoming a digital company is the same as becoming a data-driven business. In those factories, the received data is discussed in management meetings. Questions around a machine's performance are contemplated, and decisions are made based on that data. Perhaps a new machine makes a similar car part—only faster with more control over the process. The management team may discuss whether they need to invest in that new machine. All of the decisions become data driven. It is not just for technology and machinery that data is essential. Just about everything we use has sensors, from light bulbs to thermostats to phones in your hand. On the front end and back end of the company, customers provide feedback about the cars they buy. In some cases, the cars themselves send information about their performance back to the company. The data

these devices send back to a company is more powerful than any fill-in-the-blank survey."

"I have heard that data is king these days. We sell and rent equipment to construction companies around the globe. Why does data matter? All salespeople have their specific companies they work with, and they have all the data they need."

"Data is the lifeblood of a modern digital company. Digital companies use data to sense the business's state and drive real-time strategy and operational decision-making adjustments. Connected data that flows seamlessly throughout the organization is critical to the organization's success. Data does not tell you what the right answer is, but the right data at the right time, combined with the perspectives and experience of skilled staff, is what accelerates organizational performance. Many organizations are swimming in data, but that data is often incomplete or not joined up. The most critical insights often come from the correlation of disparate data sets. Transactional data for membership subscriptions, publishing revenue transactions, and event ticket sales may be helpful individually, but combining that data with behavioral data from online services and perhaps third-party data sets is likely to provide deeper insights into the trends and developing needs of the community the organization serves. Artificial intelligence models can work with that data and produce insights and connections that humans might otherwise miss. Modern digital companies invest in streamlined data capabilities and staff recruitment, training, and development with modern data analysis skills. A truly empowered culture requires an integrated foundation of operational data and front-line staff who can extract insight and value to make informed decisions."

> **"The right data at the right time ... is what accelerates organizational performance."**

"I hadn't thought about data that way."

"Becoming digital is about leveraging the power of data to make decisions and optimize businesses and processes that drive a business's success. It helps us reach customers and build the best products, and it drives the outcomes, profitability, margins, accomplishments, and more. There was a car company I worked with before working with Mod Op Strategic Consulting. Back in 2001, I ran the global account sales business at a top software company for a large car manufacturing company. I hosted their leadership team for a meeting about their new ventures. The entire conversation was about how the company was going to pivot from being an auto manufacturer to becoming a software company."

"Really?"

"They were buying up software companies left and right. They were building engineering teams to create all of this advanced technology. 2007 came along, and the auto industry got crushed, and, all of a sudden, the car company realized an important truth. They actually make cars for a living. Don't get me wrong, services are important, but services are there to build value for people who buy cars, not the other way around. In our experience, it is very easy for senior leadership teams to get distracted by a shiny object. The new software. The new computer systems. The new hardware will change everything, right? And tech is always a shiny object. It can be a huge distraction in terms of executing on your core business model."

"So this digital transformation … that is something that you can help us with? You don't think a new software platform is necessary?"

"I'm not saying it won't be a part of your overall strategy, but we would like to start with some assessments first to get to know your company and your clients. Understanding your customers' needs, what creates value for your clients, understanding your markets, understanding the competitive space that you're in—these are all essential to figure out and understand first."

"So what does this digital transformation entail?"

"We have found that a lack of clarity is problematic for senior executives charged with leading their organizations through increasingly challenging times. There's no escape from the fact that the world in which we live and operate today is digital. Transformed or not, all organizations operate in an economy where meaningful transactions and interactions with customers and stakeholders are mediated in the digital realm. The critical question for executives is not whether they can successfully drive a digital transformation but whether they can build a modern operating strategy and model that thrive in a digital world. Companies can make these changes in a high-velocity manner to keep up with their competition."

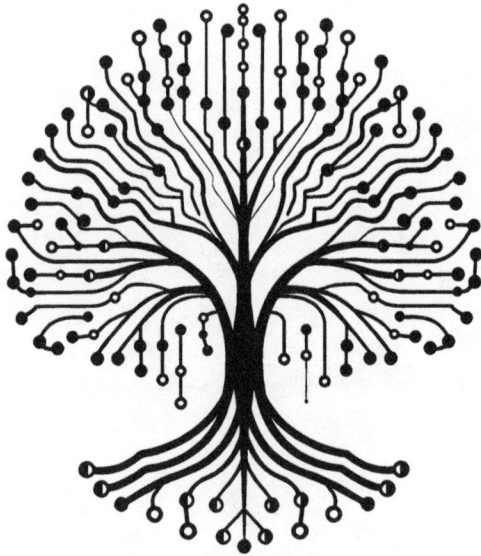

CHAPTER 2

Stage 1—Uncovering Market and Growth Opportunities

Mark and Sandra meet to discuss first steps in the process of enabling Pelican to become a digital company. Sandra still has some reservations, especially after Mark asks for access to customers and partner companies in order to contact them and get feedback about how Pelican is doing and what types of things customers are looking for. Mark explains that an outside-in approach by a third party provides the clearest and most honest response and lets Sandra know exactly how this feedback will be analyzed and how it will help Pelican identify market and growth opportunities.

Not everyone shared my view about the necessity of bringing in help so we could become a digital company. Some were less than enthralled about hiring Mod Op Strategic Consulting to help us achieve that goal. Chris, our R&D person, felt we could keep all of the projects in house to save money and not have outside consultants come in to "boss people around." I tried to assure Chris that I didn't believe that would be Mod Op Strategic Consulting's approach.

"Thank you for coming to speak with me today," I said.

"It's my pleasure. I wanted to spend today going over what to expect moving forward and to answer any questions you might have," replied Mark.

"The board and executive team are very excited to work with you all. But I'll be honest that not everyone was as positive as we are. There is a concern you are going to come in and change everything we are doing. Some feel that we are doing just fine and that funds should be allocated to new software rather than working with you."

"How do you feel about that?"

"I agree that this is a risk for the company, but a calculated one. I thought about our last meeting, and the way you described technology being a small portion of what you hope to accomplish. I agree—we need better communication with our customers. We are losing more every month, and often we have no idea why. We need a better way of working as one unit rather than individual departments doing their own thing. Am I getting this right?"

"Absolutely. We are available to discuss our process with anyone who has questions."

"I may take you up on that offer sooner rather than later."

I did some digging before the meeting. Mod Op Strategic Consulting came highly recommended by one of our top customers. Our customer told me that I would be foolish not to at least hear what they had to say. He, too, had had doubts until they shifted from sixth in their market to number two. Granted, they weren't in the industrial rental business, but they did produce forklifts and similar vehicles.

Digital growth strategy is a consistent combination of three concepts: 1) new digital products or services; 2) digital derivatives or versions of legacy products; and 3) digital enablement of legacy products through digital marketing, sales, fulfillment, and operation.

Single, large bets are very risky. Our most successful clients are those whose growth strategy enables all three elements.

Even so, I was nervous about the meeting. I heard through the grapevine that Chris wasn't the only one who thought working with consultants on digital transformation was a bad idea, even going so far as to say that it could destroy our company. I didn't subscribe to that level of negative thinking and felt like we needed to do something. Many of our competitors were doing a lot of their business online, bringing in digital marketing and AI functionality, and we were seeing a slow but steady migration of clients away from us.

Chris was right—we were still hitting our numbers, but for how long? The world in which we were operating was changing quickly, and I was afraid that maybe we were already too late.

"Based on our conversations and emails, we have come up with an initial plan of working with your organization to become a digital company. Each company we work with has its specific needs, and so we customize our approach for everyone. As you see, our first step is a growth strategy. As I mentioned last time, many of our clients have worked with other large strategy consulting firms with little to show for their invest-

ment. So we totally understand your concerns. We enable clients to develop actionable strategies that deliver tangible results. Our emphasis is on customer feedback, as this is essential to our process."

While these were some bold promises, I was supportive of their strategy.

"One of the first things we will want to do is to talk to your customers and business partners."

"You mean like sending out surveys? We do that every year, and the results are consistently positive."

"What we do goes beyond annual surveys. We want to go out and talk to them in person."

This was a bit of a jolt.

"Our customers and partners are all over the world. Are you suggesting you are going to fly all over the world and meet with them in person?"

"Yes. We find that in the early stages, it is essential to talk to customers and the companies you work alongside to help determine what their needs are, what they feel your company does right, and how things can improve."

"You don't think that surveys are enough? Flying around the world seems like an expensive proposition."

"Does your organization have a true mechanism to obtain your clients' feedback and then use that data to influence your strategic plan and offerings?"

Ouch. He had us there. We sent some of the most positive responses to team leaders by email, but that was about the extent of the use of feedback. We did share some of the negative responses as well, but it was up to the team leaders how they wanted to respond.

"Well, we don't have that exactly. We have had outstanding surveys come back. I feel we know our clients' needs. Are you sure that meeting them in person is necessary? While we want to become more digital and advance in our market, I'm afraid if we start poking around with our customers, they might think something is wrong or become irritated."

"In our experience, we have found that companies really don't know their clients' needs. You may know what they are today, and you may know what you have fixed in the past, but you may not know where to go next. I am sure those clients that replied to your surveys enjoy working with you, but we have found that those who are not happy with the services you supply often don't reply, and over time they seek services from your competitors."

"You say we should become a more digital company. Wouldn't simple video conference calls suffice?"

"It seems like that would work. But we have found people are much less distracted if we are in their presence. We don't have to call people in the middle of the night across the world. We can spend a day or two with them and get to talk to multiple people at one site. Face-to-face interviews provide us, and, in turn, you, with valuable feedback. Any digital strategy you build should be done with those you serve in mind. When you establish more authentic and regular feedback loops, you will know the areas, in real time, that you need to work on and the innovation pieces you need to develop. Not only will it make your digital strategy more on point and efficient, but your partners and customers will also love you for it."

Active engagement and input from current and prospective customers are critical to both defining and validating your market, product, and service hypotheses.

"That might be hard to sell to the board and executive team. The argument will be that our sales projections are good this year, so why are we bothering our clients?"

"You provided us with your sales projections, and, yes, your numbers look good at the moment. But we looked at who some of your competition is. They are moving ahead and producing digital products and services. They are already becoming digital companies. This is not just about technology; they are leading in customer satisfaction, and within a couple of years, we feel that falling behind much further could hurt your company's bottom line significantly. Your industry is becoming more automated every year. AI is absorbing some of the most expensive functions and allowing huge leaps in others. Marketing is becoming more data-dependent. You need to adapt or you could become obsolete."

Another ouch moment. I didn't like to think that Pelican could become obsolete. But having Mod Op Strategic Consulting touch base with our customers and partner sites seemed extreme.

"I don't know; it sounds expensive. We have clients and partners worldwide. The expenses could stack up quickly. Even I haven't met with many of our customers."

Mark raised an eyebrow. It's true, I hadn't met with many of our partners or customers. We had exchanged calls or emails, but I hadn't spoken to them in person. I didn't believe anyone in our company had met some of our biggest, longest-standing customers in person. He had a point. We weren't doing a great job knowing our customers better.

"In our experience, you will waste more money adding digital components that you don't need and that your customers don't want than if you have their input from the beginning. In the end, it not only will save your budget, but your customers will notice your efforts to improve your digital interface with them."

"I suppose that makes sense. How long will the process of meeting with customers take?"

If this was their process, and we were going to hire them, then we had to trust they knew what they were doing. Our relationships with our customers were very transactional. But Mark was right; it was shortsighted to think that we knew what our customers wanted from us. We were assuming a lot.

"It will take a few weeks. You will appreciate the results, I promise you."

"You're that confident about your outcomes?"

"Yes. We want to see you succeed. This is not a one-and-done situation. If you hurry the process and leave parts out, it doesn't go well. We have seen companies fail miserably."

"What if we sent some of our own people to talk to our customers? You can give them a list of questions. They already have established relationships with our customers, and it might be less invasive and awkward."

"Eliciting feedback from internal sources isn't always reliable. Sometimes salespeople hear what they want to hear. If a client likes a salesperson, they are less likely to complain and be truthful. Whether you use us or someone else, you are better off using an outside source for feedback if you want the straight scoop from your clients."

All customer insight can be useful, but relying on any one type, at the expense of direct interviews with customers and prospects by an expert third party, can blunt or slant the feedback, making it less useful for strategic and product guidance.

Suboptimal Approaches for Customer Insight

- **Sales leaders as proxies for the Voice of the Customer**. Often, customers let their personal feelings toward a good salesperson keep them from providing honest feedback.

- **Founders and company leaders as proxies for the Voice of the Customer**. Even if they came from the market and once knew it well, anyone working at a company becomes susceptible to inside-out thinking, and this can keep them from hearing new opportunities, etc.

- **Internally conducted interviews with customers**. Internal interviews can be very useful, particularly when you have a new product that you want to test and gather feedback on. However, internal people come with their own prejudices and can easily let those thoughts taint an interview, asking leading questions and generally trying to prove the point they want to prove rather than truly hearing what the customer is saying.

- **Net Promoter Score (NPS) as a proxy for the Voice of the Customer.** NPS is a very useful metric, and anyone who has answered a survey with a 1–10 rating on whether they would recommend a product or service knows it matters. But it shouldn't be your only metric. And NPS works less well for B2B products and services. We have found that intent to purchase services again is a better leading indicator than NPS.

I had to think about that for a moment. And it made sense. Did I really know what my clients wanted or needed? Would they complain about something or just move on to another company? In the early days, I had a better sense of my clients because there were fewer of us in the business, and I was more involved with the clients. I relied on the sales team now, and while they were good, Mark was right. I couldn't know for sure if I was getting honest, helpful feedback. It seemed like the investment in having the group go out and talk to our clients would be less costly than losing any more key customers.

"What do you do when you meet customers?"

"When we meet with your customers, we go in as a neutral party. We are not offended by what they say, so we encourage them to be brutally honest, and we are in a position to ask the hard questions. The other thing we don't do is ask leading questions. We find most companies we have worked with ask leading questions because they have their own priorities, and they want their customer feedback to support their priorities."

Again, the logic was sound, so why was I so reluctant? If I was being honest with myself, it was because I wasn't sure I wanted to know the truth. People say they want to know what a person thinks or feels, but do we really? Also, cost was something to consider, and what if they didn't bring back any information we didn't already know?

"I will need to go to my executive team and board with some numbers, because I know they are going to ask how much this is going to cost and what the return on the investment will be."

"It would be difficult for us or any other firm to determine how you should build your digital company without clearly knowing what the customer's needs are. We would be guessing and potentially missing the mark. The return is that it allows us to partner with you and make clear goals and strategies that will work. For instance, wouldn't it be nice to have client feedback assigned to a product so that you can see that your product road maps are being driven by client priorities? Well-governed digital companies do that. Client data and feedback are central

> **"Client data and feedback are central to driving the prioritization of what gets done in the product workstream."**

to driving the prioritization of what gets done in the product workstream. These are some of the fundamental things that make a digital company successful. Your salespeople probably know your clients very well and have good relationships with them, but that doesn't mean you have good insight into what your clients are going to value or think is important to them in rank priority. Being able to have a solid feedback loop with your clients will help you make decisions about which products and services to build and how you should adjust your business model. That's a different level of analysis, but you need to have clear data to support it."

I appreciated his forthright, no-nonsense approach, but it was making my stomach twist a little bit.

"How will this help us compete better in the marketplace?"

"That is a great question. The feedback we receive will help drive the future road map for your company. This will help you create strategies that will not only help you catch up to your competition but will also give you a clearer idea of where you can expand products and innovate new ones, and also how to market the products and services you already have. First, you need to gather and then analyze the feedback you receive. We help do that for you. We will then come back to you with that data, and we can begin to create a road map moving forward."

YOUR MARKET IS CHANGING
Are you prepared to respond and lead?

In today's economy, digital innovation is rapidly changing traditional markets, disrupting relationships between customers and suppliers while creating new opportunities for forward-thinking businesses.

With virtually all transactions conducted digitally or driven by digital components, executives are increasingly seeking to understand the fundamental shifts of how digital innovation is impacting the way their markets operate and the strategies that can deliver new customers, new relationships, and new growth opportunities in this changing landscape.

Market Mapping—unlock your full potential with this five-step framework:

STEP 1: MAPPING THE MARKET—Who serves your customers?

- Identify customer segments and service providers who sell to those segments
- Create visual "maps" that put each customer segment in the center and show the connectivity with the service providers

STEP 2: CURRENT MARKET POSITION—Where do you currently play?

- Identify which verticals you play in now and with what products and services
- Identify verticals that represent your strongest growth opportunities

STEP 3: MAXIMIZING CURRENT BUSINESS—The "inside" opportunities

- Dive deep into the current business and evaluate
- Identify new opportunities using research, surveys, and interviews with customers and users of the key products and services

STEP 4: NEW OPPORTUNITIES IN THE MARKET—The "outside" opportunities

- Outside-in research, market sizing, players, competitors, partners, and best-practice examples, augmented with customer and prospect surveys and interviews
- Validate based on Market Need, Right to Play, Revenue Potential, Mission Alignment, and Executional Difficulty

STEP 5: CHOOSING THE BEST OPTIONS—What should you prioritize?

- Synthesize the inside-out, outside-in, and other research, validated with customer surveys and/or interviews
- Deliver a discrete set of prioritized opportunities with summary business cases

A deeper understanding of existing and new market opportunities is the bedrock of any growth plan. Market mapping allows you to:

- Map opportunities in existing, adjacent, new, or redefined markets
- Identify new or derivative products and services to meet emerging market and customer demands
- Consider how developing new customer experiences could retain existing customers and attract new customers

An **"inside-out" evaluation** analyzes your existing products, services, and customers and positions them within your core markets. In this process we interview customers and staff to understand your current state and consider potential in-line growth opportunities.

An **"outside-in" exploration** seeks to expand your growth potential beyond the core by exploring opportunities within the broader market ecosystem. We identify and prioritize products, services, technologies, and organizations in market "white spaces" that offer truly incremental opportunities for growth.

"We are currently in the top 5 percent of our market. How can this help us do better?"

"Do you know whether your competition sells goods and services similar to the ones you do?"

"Yes."

"What other goods and services do people buy from your competitors that you don't offer?"

I had to think about that for a moment.

"They offer new and used equipment sales, maintenance, and on-site delivery. To be honest, I'm not completely sure."

"Part of our meetings with your clients is to help reveal these sorts of products and services. Knowing this can help you grow your business and lead to new innovations."

This came back to the type of relationships we have with our clients. While we asked whether our clients liked our services and what we could improve, we didn't ask them about other possible services that they might want.

"This information helps us in planning your digital strategies. We're interested in what your clients do right before they use your product or service and what they do right after. Those are often opportunities for additional products and services that you can offer because your client is already in the workflow at that particular moment."

I was realizing that not only could Mod Op Strategic Consulting help us become a digital company, but they could also help our overall growth. This project had a larger scope than I thought it would.

"We can help you see your company and what you offer from your customers' point of view. Sure, it will mean more work to add those things they might suggest, but they are already part of the overall workflow. If we can help you better understand what that workflow looks like, we can help make recommendations about new opportunities for your company."

"We have a number of new products and services we are working on. We just haven't been able to pull the trigger yet. Can you help us with launching those new innovations?"

"That is another reason we want to talk to your customers. We have worked with other companies that had a very specific idea of what they could be doing in the marketplace. They thought nobody else was doing what they were considering and that if they could pull it off, it would be huge. As you said, they were working on those ideas but could never quite get them to market. We did what we call market mapping with their prospects and customers. We asked them if the company deployed the new product or service, what the value would be to them. What we found was that people would not pay for the new product. But while they weren't interested in spending money on that product, they were interested in something adjacent to it."

Saving money and not wasting it on innovations our customers didn't want was going to be a big selling point for the executive team.

"So what happened to those companies?"

"We came back and redefined their focus and were able to work on ideas that their customers actually wanted."

"Tell me more about your market mapping approach."

"It begins with the face-to-face interviews with your customers and partners. We dig into what you are offering or could offer in the future.

We ask questions like these: Do you like this? Is this worth the money? Does this help you in your workflow? What did you do before? What did you do after? Where else would you go for this? If you can't get it, what do you do? Getting that direct feedback is hugely valuable.

"Once we have a better understanding of your company and those you serve, we can create a structured road map moving forward. We can develop hypotheses of things that need to improve in your company and test out new product and service ideas before determining whether they are things that will work in your company.

"Some of the ideas we will test may be ideas and projects you have tried in the past. We will dive into why they may not have worked before and what you can do to try again with a better chance of success. We can also evaluate projects you are working on now and determine if they need to be tweaked, or even scrapped."

"You suggest companies scrap projects they have invested time and money in?"

"We can test them out and determine first if they are things that your customers want and will pay for. There is no sense in continuing to devote resources to projects that will not only have no return but could turn your customers toward competitors who are providing what they want."

While it made my stomach hurt to stop projects we had invested hundreds of thousands of dollars in, it didn't make sense to chase bad money with good. I hope there weren't too many areas we would have to overhaul, but I was open to the ideas they would present.

In order to grow, we needed to try new ideas, even if we failed.

"Do you have any other questions before we send our full proposal to you?"

"Not at the moment, but I'm sure my executive team will have many questions along the way."

"We will be available and accessible anytime you need to ask questions."

I knew what Mod Op Strategic Consulting was offering would be considered a risky proposition to some within our company. My belief was it would be riskier not to become digital. It occurred to me that as a company, perhaps we had become complacent. We had become too comfortable with our success and were unwilling to jeopardize that and take any risks. In order to grow, we needed to try new ideas, even if we failed. With no risk, there would be no returns.

***

WHAT DOES THIS MEAN FOR YOU?

As a CEO, your efforts should be focused on getting the buy-in and support you need internally to drive change and getting honest feedback from your customers and markets. This feedback must then be focused around the three growth elements.

1. New digital products or services

2. Digital derivatives or versions of legacy products

3. Digital enablement of legacy products through digital marketing, sales, fulfillment, and operation

When receiving feedback, put yourself in the shoes of the customers and look at things from the outside in to develop as unbiased a picture as possible.

CHECKLIST

- **Get buy-in**—Gain the support you need from other executives and your board by identifying capability needs.

- **Project plan**—Create a laundry list of all tasks that need to be completed over time.

- **Feedback loop**—Identify a resource or team to "own" the collection of first-person customer insight. This can be internal or external to your organization.

- **Market assessment**—Work with your executive team to build a market map of your key markets and use it to help identify new opportunities.

TOOL KIT

- **Project plan**—Set the tasks to be completed over time, and assign them owners and priorities.

- **Categorize feedback**—Use tools available to break down and categorize market and customer feedback.

- **Market map**—Create a view of the world that puts your customer at the epicenter and all of the goods and services available around them. This will help you find "white space."

LESSONS LEARNED

- The best time to transform your business is when things are going well. Don't wait until sales and other metrics are on the downswing.

- The best time to transform your business is when things are going well. Don't wait until sales and other metrics are on the downswing.

- It is critical to take the time to obtain and use customer and prospect feedback, leveraging data, interviews, and other feedback to establish or validate hypotheses about customer needs. And it is essential to get the customer feedback from the customers themselves rather than relying on salespeople, SMEs, and even your own views as proxies for customers.

- Building a market map of what types of products and services your customers buy, and from whom, can help identify parts of the market that you are not serving but perhaps could be.

RESOURCES

- https://dprism.com/insights/
  five-steps-to-unlocking-market-opportunities/

- https://dprism.com/insights/
  mapping-your-market-to-get-a-sense-of-where-you-are/

CHAPTER 3

Stage 2—Formulating a Strategy, Prioritizing, and Assessing Capabilities

Three months after Mod Op Strategic Consulting began its work with Pelican, Sandra and Mark discuss the report with feedback from customers and business partners. This is an eye-opening session for Sandra. She is both shocked and encouraged. This is a process of discovery, meeting with the customers and other stakeholders in the company. Mod Op Strategic Consulting spent time recording, transcribing, and then organizing those interviews. They presented their findings and thoughts about where the gaps may be in how Pelican is serving its clients and the new capabilities needed to organize and harness the power of the data flowing through the business. Mark explains that it is common for people to be either overexcited, naysayers, or pragmatic, the last of which falls somewhere in the middle. Mod Op Strategic Consulting's goal is to take a pragmatic approach and get buy-in from everyone. All of those pieces and parts must run smoothly together in order to create a digital strategy that works.

"We are so glad you were open to us working with you and your customers these past few months," Mark said. "We have been able to gain a lot of great insights into the current state of your company and plenty of ideas about the opportunities sitting in front of you. As we move forward, we can assess more deeply the current state of data and digital capabilities and where you can improve and potentially innovate. We feel like we have some great feedback to help develop a road map for the future.

"This is really only the beginning. We are going to present you with our findings and give you our interpretations of the data. We won't immediately jump into strategies because we need to develop some hypotheses to test out with you. The process of testing and working through hypotheses will be ongoing as we move forward and jointly find new opportunities that need to be explored.

"Developing a data strategy requires you to develop a deep understanding and sense of the value of data to the organization. A good data strategy helps you move forward, it helps the business at large understand the importance of data in creating value, and it drives consensus around the direction and investments needed to move forward. Data strategy is not simply about reducing the risk or implementing governance. An effective data strategy integrates a wide range of factors: the goals of the business and product teams, the capabilities and workflow of the analytics and engineering teams, the health of existing systems and data resources, and the entire process of how the life cycle of data assets are managed for the business. In today's world, data is as important an asset as cash and it needs to be managed with the same care. That's particularly true with the coming potential of AI—which fundamentally depends on a solid foundation of trusted and curated data. Without well-managed data, you cannot hope to leverage the power of new AI tools as they become available."

"That is a lot to take in," I said.

"Yes, it can be a lot, and, hopefully, it will make much more sense by

the end of our discussion today. My meeting with you today is preliminary. We will have similar meetings with each of your team leaders."

I hoped those meetings would go well. There had been a lot of talk the past few months as Mod Op Strategic Consulting's team met with many of our customers worldwide. All of the feedback we received from those customers was positive. However, Chris, our head of R&D, was still having issues with Mod Op's presence. I continued to reinforce that Mark and his team had my full support and that we were moving forward with them.

"Before you is a report of the key areas that came up in our interviews. We have collated all of the interviews into one report with some of the more important responses. We are also providing you with a spreadsheet of all of the answers individually."

I had looked over the report briefly before my meeting with Mark and was blown away by what our customers had to say—both positive and negative. Some of the areas they talked about, such as their frustrations with our current billing system, were eye opening.

"What kinds of questions did you ask?"

"The report is a collated collection of all the questions and responses. We recorded all of our interviews and then had them transcribed. You can read the actual questions and responses together. It might be helpful for you to see those responses, and we have organized it all in a searchable database so that they are easy to read and understand."

"I anticipate some of the leaders will jump on this and demand we update our outdated software capabilities. I also believe some of them will challenge the responses you received."

"Both of those are valid reactions. We know there will be excitement and anxiety about what these reports mean, but we aren't suggesting overwhelming changes today. We will work with your teams to break down the data we gathered and discuss how to prioritize new projects. There

isn't a quick fix, especially since we haven't quite yet identified what needs fixing. This is merely the first step."

"As I am reading through this, I believe most of it is true, but we can't solve everything overnight. I agree we need to make sure we are solving the right things. We have budget, time, and resource constraints to consider. I think it is an excellent idea for you to meet with each department individually."

"Data, specifically data management, is the lifeblood of a digital company."

"Once we have gone through that process, we can come back together and decide how to proceed as a company. We have the input from your customers. This is an outside-in approach. Now we need to help you develop new strategies from the inside out. This takes time, and it takes input from everyone. This is your company, and you know what is best in your market and field of expertise. Our job is to help guide you on the path to becoming a more automated and data-informed business.

"Here is a snapshot of areas that we feel are some of the biggest feedback points. This is aggregated from our observations during our interviews. You will also see our priority drivers. These are the greatest needs that came out of the feedback, specifically pointed toward your company becoming more digital."

"There seems to be a lot of emphasis on data."

"That's a great observation. Data, specifically data management, is the lifeblood of a digital company. It is not just in IT or any particular department. Like blood, data is pumped to all the parts of your company, from how you market your products and services and generate new leads, through how you sell and build client relationships, through to the delivery of products and the after-sales service. It should all operate as one connected business—with data providing the connection.

The importance of data and how to use it effectively is changing the very fabric of many companies, with chief data officers (CDOs) becoming increasingly important and reporting to CIOs, CTOs, CDOs, or even CEOs in some organizations.

While we have a lot of data in today's marketplace, the value is not the data itself. The value comes from data insights, which inherently find themselves in the data science part of the equation.

Data science begins with a vision and a belief—the belief that data is a critical asset for your organization, with almost equal importance to cash. This is true for virtually every digitally driven business.

Recognizing the critical value of your data assets empowers your team to make the right investments of time, energy, and resources.

"I know there are some leaders who will want to know what new technology we plan to add and implement."

"*Technology is a part of that process, but we aim to first decide the best ways to use the data. Once we can help determine that, then we can help you pick the right technological strategies that can help you achieve those goals.*

"*We will help you create a strategic framework. You see your priority drivers. Those will be validated in the next phase of work we will do with you once we have had a chance to work with each department. We want to make sure these align with everyone. Once those have been determined, then we can help you with the required capabilities to move those drivers, with the expected outcomes on the other end.*"

Identifying the needs of the business required for today and anticipated for tomorrow is the biggest factor in creating a business strategy to guide a new data platform. Consider the following questions at the beginning of the upgrade initiative: What are you trying to achieve as an organization? What are the problems you are trying to solve? What is the value of data inside the organization? What needles are you trying to move?

It's from the perspective of well-defined business goals that current architectural deficiencies can be understood and from which a modern data strategy and data platform road map can begin to take shape.

"In order to compete with other companies, we have developed some comparisons. We compare some of the leading practices in your industry with the feedback we collected while speaking to your clients. This has helped us develop a list of required capabilities. This is a place to start— and, again, we will dive deeper into these in our individual sessions. We focus on people, process, and technology, as these enable you to accomplish your business goals."

"This is the kind of information that I believe will help us grow our business into the future. What we did so far to build the company was great, but we need new strategies to grow and compete in the digital space. This creates a great road map to accomplish that."

"Because few organizations have the luxury of building a modern data platform from scratch, a progressive, pragmatic approach is most effective. Projects are the incremental steps toward building a data platform, one slice at a time. Solve the most important problems first. This approach allows organizations to keep the lights on, easily track returns on investments, and begin to work out which new products may

be attractive and when. As new projects launch, with more capabilities in place, the velocity of project execution will improve.

"We match your capabilities with the corresponding strategic actions and tactical actions. Strategic actions are things that have an extended life and are more complicated in that they require executive sign-off and may require a substantial investment justification to actually bring life to those strategies. Those are actions that require more than a single organization to make a decision and get on with it. The tactical actions are things you are already doing but are also things that you can tweak and improve, perhaps with the help of AI. These are things that can be accomplished, and decisions made concerning, without executive oversight."

"This is all supported by the interviews you conducted?"

I had underestimated how the data from the interviews could be leveraged and how it could be transferred into actionable items.

"Yes. You can read verbatim what was said in the spreadsheet we have provided. The responses are collated so that you can easily read what was said in reference to the different areas we have presented."

Effective digital transformations require a clear strategic framework for the business to guide prioritization and decision-making.

"We have already completed our kickoff, interviews, and analysis. Next we will work on the framework and growth hypothesis as I have described. We will discuss what we have discovered and come up with some of those strategies, which we will then test out. If, for instance, we believe that you need a better way to track your inventory, we will come up with possible strategies for doing that, and then decide as a group how to best tackle that project. Once we have had a chance to refine those strategies,

we will reconvene and discuss how all those parts will work together and develop a budget and schedule to begin putting them into action."

"So the recommendations you are presenting to the teams aren't the final recommendations?"

"No, these are our hypotheses based on the interviews and other data we have gathered about your industry. These are suggestions based on our experiences and on our comparative analysis. In order to come up with a framework that will work with your organization, we will need to work with your teams to validate our hypotheses.

"With transformations occurring in every corner of the data and analytics ecosystem, the incremental approach makes sense for most organizations. The initial steps of this approach address the essential components that must go into building a modern data architecture, among them data security, governance, and master data management. Two other components stand out as especially crucial to the long-term value of the architecture: capabilities supporting data as a service, and developing a real-time infrastructure. This takes time to work through. So we hope to establish clear expectations with your teams."

> Knowing where to start and what to prioritize in a digital transformation requires a baseline understanding of the organization's current technology, data, process, and skills capabilities.

"On average how long does the process take?"

"It varies. Each company and each strategy is unique to that company. We don't use a one-size-fits-all approach with this. We want to help you create solutions that will work and that can permeate the greater culture of the company. Our goal is to help you to become digital. We are offering you the tools and our inputs, but we need help to get to where you want

to go. You are the experts in your business, and so you know better what has worked in the past. All we ask is that you have an open mind to some other possibilities that you have not tried or that you may have tried in the past and failed. It may not be the idea that didn't work. It might have been the execution or maybe the lack of the proper resources.

"I know that's a long answer to a short question, but at this stage, it is hard to say until we meet with you in our sessions. Then we can get a better sense of how long that process might take. Some strategies we may be able to implement right away with total agreement, while others may take months to develop."

> **We would figure out the strategies and means to make it happen at a pace we could handle.**

A weight was lifted from my shoulders. We would have a plan all the leaders would be involved with, and these folks would connect these data streams together for the entire company. Then we would figure out the strategies and means to make it happen at a pace we could handle.

We have had other consulting companies work with us over the years. They had great ideas, wonderful reports, and charts. At the end of the day, we might have had a playbook, but that usually ended with the executive team. We didn't know how to implement the changes, and we didn't have the right people on board to do it.

"Once those strategies are agreed upon, what can we expect during implementation?"

"We can help you decide what you can do in house and then figure out what outside resources you may need. We can also help with the governance of those projects should that be valuable to you.

"Modern data platforms need to be geared for real-time or near-real-

time capabilities to support the movement of data and the results of data analysis to decision-makers and to customers at the right time that they're needed. Whether it's predictive analytics coming from a data warehouse, a recommendation based on an analysis of streaming behavioral data from a website, or a robust AI-based support system answering common customer questions with real-time language processing, the ability to act on this information in real time will be a distinguishing feature of leading brands. We will be there to help you find the right resources to do this. Some we may be able to do in house, while for others we will make recommendations to you. The important thing about the execution stage is that you have a governance plan in place. We have seen a number of companies develop some great strategies only for it all to fall apart because there was not someone governing the project's execution."

"You have given me a lot to think about. I'd like to be at the meetings you have with the leaders and teams so that I can understand it better as we go through the process."

"Sounds like an excellent idea!"

***

WHAT DOES THIS MEAN FOR YOU?

Now that you have collected invaluable feedback from customers, you can focus your attention inward to understand where your capabilities are and where those capabilities fall short in achieving your future goals. These capabilities fall into the general categories of people, process, and technology and will form the foundational elements for a road map to accomplish transformation.

With so much new information coming from the "outside in," you must maintain an objective view in order to see all of the possibilities. As it turns out, this is an executive's opportunity to help bring the senior leadership together to come up with the important next steps in order to get to a forward-looking strategy.

CHECKLIST

- **Capability assessment**—Commission a capability assessment to identify gaps between your current state and desired future state. (This can be internal or external depending on your capacity and resources.) Process maps are a good tool to employ during this process.

- **Executive forum**—Create a forum with your executive team specifically to discuss these strategic, transformational issues. We have found that it is essential for these meetings to be distinct from your day-to-day operational discussions. An outside facilitator can help ensure that these meetings stay outwardly focused.

- **Review feedback**—Get comfortable with the feedback you have gotten from your customers and internalize what this might mean from a needs perspective.

- **Data strategy**—Lay out a vision for employing data as it relates to capabilities and decision-making. What rules are required to manage your organization's physical and digital assets? This is your vision for collecting, storing, sharing, and using your data.

TOOL KIT

- **Process maps**—Identify a resource or team to "own" the collection of conversations detailing all of your organization's processes. What do these look like end-to-end today, and what should they look like in the future? This is part of your capability assessment.

- **Strategic framework**—Create a model that visualizes your capability assessment. How does it show where you are today versus where you need to be tomorrow? How do your people, process, and technology play a role in this future? This document will remain your "North Star," which can be tweaked as new information becomes available.

LESSONS LEARNED

- When embarking on a digital transformation, it is critical to establish a baseline of current capabilities and to identify gaps, and therefore investments, that need to be made.

- CEO and C-suite engagement and buy-in on strategic frameworks and the priorities behind them are essential.

- Don't expect to arrive at a definitive strategic "answer" in one cycle. Develop a range of hypotheses that can be tested, validated, and prioritized.

RESOURCES

- https://dprism.com/insights/technology-assessment-steps/
- https://dprism.com/insights/technology-system-misconceptions/
- https://dprism.com/insights/portfolio-management-technology-strategy/
- https://dprism.com/insights/todays-investors-demand-bullet-proof-digital-strategies-prepared/

CHAPTER 4

Creating a Platform Strategy and a Technology Road Map

"You'll be happy to know we will be talking about technology today!" Mark said.

"That is great news. I understand a bit better now that technology is not the primary focus of digital transformation," I replied.

"But make no mistake, technology is definitely a part of it. As I have said before, data is the lifeblood of a digital company, so technology is essential to manage the life cycle of that data and to ensure you have appropriate controls over this critical asset. The old way of managing the business via email and dealing with paper invoices is in your rearview mirror."

"Mostly in our rearview mirror. We have some folks still using a fax machine, but we are working with them on it. It isn't that they don't have the technology available to them. It is more that they are reluctant to change from the way we processed orders in the past."

"That is why we have really worked hard in having you define how you want these processes to work in your organization. Technology is only as good as what it is being used for, and bigger and more expensive is not always the answer."

"Our board is glad to hear that."

"Successful digital businesses depend on fully integrated data and technology platform capabilities. The idea is that many of the things that are being manually keyed are automated. And, more importantly, the data should be easy to analyze and up to date. As the CEO, you should know what is happening in any part of your company at any time."

> **"Technology is only as good as what it is being used for."**

"That sounds wonderful, and I believe we are getting there. I'm just anxious to know how technology will help us achieve that."

"We have been helping you define your platform because it is critical to enabling your transformation. We are identifying the technology gaps and the capabilities that need to be aligned with them. These are driven by your strategic business and product priorities. Through this process, we arrive at a road map. It is there that we begin to think about new or upgraded technologies like using cloud computing, new insights and analytics capabilities, and artificial intelligence moving forward. We identify not only the need but also the capabilities required to create and run it."

"So will we need a complete overhaul of our technology platform?"

"Not necessarily. Like many other companies we work with, you have a relatively traditional technology landscape. You've invested in your specific set of technology capabilities and solutions for the thirty years you've been in business. This includes your finance system, manufacturing production control system, sales and customer management system, and

everything else. These technologies were dependent on the decisions made by your business.

"Those decisions were rational, intelligent choices at the time and were geared toward a specific set of needs for a specific defined function in the business to solve a particular set of business challenges.

"Those decisions were based on needs driven by a very inside-out perspective, needs such as selling more to your customers, which created the need for a customer relationship management system. You needed to manage your inventory better; therefore, you upgraded your inventory control system. You needed to manage sales and revenue better, so you re-tooled your finance system, right?"

"You're spot on."

"In today's world, if you are going to be a digital company serving your clients through digital self-service capabilities, then the set of needs that your technology strategy has to enable are not your needs, but the customer's needs."

"That's an interesting perspective … go on."

"That's the important pivot. Generally, your customers' needs are materially different from your needs. Some of the most important ways they're different are that your customers have grown up in a world where they're used to using very sophisticated digital services that answer questions at the touch of a button. They no longer need to go to the bank to handle their account. They can see all of their statements online. The same is true of their insurance company—they can view their policy and even get a digital version of their insurance card on their phone. Customers' needs are in mind when they visit one of those companies online. Their digital presence is designed to anticipate the needs of their consumer. Consider a company like Uber. Their platform is set up to anticipate the need for a car service or to get a package from A to B. Their entire digital experience is designed to optimize and fulfill that need, right? And the marketing

these businesses direct toward their customers speaks to those same needs, not the needs of the company."

> Remember the outside-in-versus-inside-out perspective from chapter 2? The same concept applies here when thinking about future technology.

"I understand where you are coming from, and you are right. Most of our technology has been to help us internally with little thought of how that would serve our customers' needs."

"That is one of the reasons we interview your clients at the beginning of our work with you—to see their needs. But it doesn't stop with that initial contact. You will continue that conversation with them regularly."

"I have to admit I was a little afraid when you first mentioned interviewing so many of them, but I can more clearly see now why you did that, and the information you brought back was gold!"

"The material difference from a technology strategy is that your customers' needs don't view your business as a set of functional silos. Instead, they require your organization to work as one company. Suppose your client needs bulldozers at a site in Germany. They want to visit your digital service and see what equipment is available in your inventory management system. They want to know the price for leasing the bulldozers for the next three months. That's your finance system. Then they need to order the equipment to their specifications—that's in your customer relationship management system. And then they need to transact back to your finance system and get their order fulfilled—that is your operations system. They might need something else, too, maybe even something they don't yet realize—and that's where artificial intelligence can play a role. Your client doesn't care to know that you have five or six different systems serving that need. They want a seamlessly integrated experience."

"And that's what we are creating?"

"Yes, that's what we are creating."

"I can see now why we didn't start with the technology piece. We didn't really have a clear understanding of what our clients needed or wanted."

"Precisely. This has huge implications on the type of technology architecture that is chosen. The technology architecture must pivot from being functionally focused on solving the needs of a particular business unit to being horizontally integrated to serve the connected needs of a client who must join up all of those bits of your business to deliver the experience they are looking for.

"And that's where the platform comes in. It's a means of abstracting all of that underlying complexity and presenting it to the outside world as a connected and joined-up set of services."

"So all these parts have to be interconnected internally within the company?"

"Your technology platform is either a replacement for or a layer on top of your existing technology platform. In your case, we suggest a mixture of layering a platform on top of what you already have and adding some new components."

"That's a relief, because the board has been concerned that you would suggest a wholesale replacement of everything."

"That isn't always the best way to go, not only from a financial perspective but also from a change management one. We are careful not to throw out the baby with the bathwater."

Both of us chuckled at that.

"The idea is to build a platform that provides an integrational layer across all of those older systems and makes them look like one integrated service or a set of integrated services to your customers."

"I like it!"

"In these days of cloud services, you can adjust your service level depending on the volume of clients you're dealing with at any point in time, and you can make your service available reliably at scale. That's 365 days a year without interruption. And where humans have a limited window of availability, or limited bandwidth to do everything a customer may want, that's where AI can come in.

"So this isn't just about the capabilities we are working on now?"

"Our goal is to make you independent so that you can create new innovations and repeat the process we have laid out for you.

"Consider that you will soon have a great idea for a new service that you want to bring to market. Once you have the platform in place, instead of having to go back and customize and integrate all of those individual functional capabilities, you now have a way to easily bring all of that together. You can build on top of the platform services. And that platform has already figured out how to integrate all of your business's capabilities on the back end."

"So a sort of plug-and-play approach?"

"You get it. The analogy I like to use is LEGO building blocks. The platform provides a foundation; you can use building blocks to construct new services. Many websites are built with modules; you can add new modules as needed and take others away when they no longer serve your clients. Modern enterprises think about their internal enterprise architecture being able to do the same thing because, ultimately, these platform strategies are generally invested in based on ROI from better customer service, more effective marketing, better revenue flow, getting new services to market, and more. When you've got a solid platform, you can build better tools and internal capabilities for the organization, and you're able to do it much faster."

"If our competitors use many of the same tools and capabilities, won't our companies look cookie-cutter? I have seen other industries like credit card companies where it is hard to tell one company from another."

"That's not the fault of the platform. That's an indication of a lack of innovation inside the organization. There's a maturity curve. You start with having no platform at all. Suppose you don't have a platform strategy today, and you have a demand from your customers to deliver new services. In that case, you're at a significant technical and business disadvantage to any other players in your market who can do that. So that's level one. Platform is the price of entry to meet customer expectations.

"The second thing is, once you have a platform, what are you building on top of it? How are you differentiating? Consider Ford and GM. They're basically selling the same product. They sell trucks with four wheels, with a bed and different variations of cabs. At face value, 80 to 90 percent of what a truck is today is the same whether you buy it from Ford, GM, Dodge, or whoever. The 10 percent or 20 percent of the space where they innovate makes the difference between whether somebody buys one brand or another. Not to mention the marketing—which we at Mod Op can absolutely help with once we get the platform up and running.

"What is that 20 percent difference? Maybe I need more towing capacity, or perhaps I want the most luxurious interior. It could be that I want a generator built in and to be able to charge things in my truck bed because I'm running a job site and I need to run equipment. Those are the 20 percent requirements that go beyond, and that's where competition ends up in the truck business. It's also where the competition is in your industry as well. Innovation taps into those areas of differentiation based on your client's needs and that can then be layered over your platform."

"I think I get it."

"Let me put it a different way. Platform isn't what levels the playing field. It's the price of entry to be in the game. Suppose you don't move beyond the price of admission. In that case, you're unlikely to be success-

ful, or you're unlikely to satisfy your customers, or you're unlikely to grab new market share from your competitors because you're just like everybody else, or worse.

"That's where the alignment to strategy comes in. We are working to help you figure out the highest priorities of your company, which are driven by your clients' preferences. That is why we are building a road map to prioritize these capabilities."

"It's a lot to think about, but I believe I have a better understanding of the technology piece and can assure the board we aren't going to have to overhaul everything. Instead, we can decide what we need to add based on our platform now and be flexible in the future as new demands for innovation come from our clients' needs."

***

WHAT DOES THIS MEAN FOR YOU?

As you move toward your digital transformation, remember that your technology and data are primarily set up for you to fulfill your customer's needs—this is what you are enabling. This is a cultural shift in the way your organization conducts business, effectively shifting from an inside-out approach to an outside-in perspective.

CHECKLIST

- **Future state**—Envision and define your future state in terms of outcomes and capabilities.

- **Gap analysis**—Assess your process, talent, and technology gaps stopping you from getting to your future state.

- **Technology architecture**—Define and draw your technology schema to identify key platforms, processes, and data needs.

- **Artificial Intelligence**—Figure out where AI can add value and how to incorporate it into various elements of the platform.

TOOL KIT

- Undertake a baseline assessment/diagnostic and gap analysis of the organization's current technology landscape, skills, and vendor relationships.

- Define a future state platform architecture designed to enable the strategic outcomes defined for the transformation strategy and to maximize the velocity of turning ideas into new revenue-generating products in front of customers.

- Align the gap analysis with future-state platform architecture and the key strategic transformation priorities to develop an investment road map maintaining a clear focus on the delivery of early value to the business.

LESSONS LEARNED

- Successful digital companies depend on horizontal integration across the business, ensuring a seamless flow of information and decision-making. Traditional application silos that are hard to integrate no longer suffice.

- Data is the lifeblood of a digital business. The walls between islands of data have to be taken down to ensure that the business has a 360-degree view of customers, their needs, and the operational performance of the organization.

- Having the internal skills to define the required platform and data architecture and to manage the technical decision-making will ultimately be required.

RESOURCES

- https://dprism.com/insights/digital-platform-strategy/
- https://dprism.com/insights/planning-your-digital-future-under-the-covid-sun/

CHAPTER 5

Planning for Execution

"I really appreciate you taking the time to meet with me. One of the key aspects of the transformation of a company is that there is support from the CEO and executive team. This is especially true in this phase of the project, which is reviewing our findings from talking with your customers and beginning to work with your teams to test our hypothesis about what projects should be considered and what prioritization might look like," Mark said.

I was excited to get started and a bit nervous. In the past couple of weeks, I had received three types of responses from my team leaders. The first was exuberant enthusiasm—people were ready to get started. No matter the cost to the company, they didn't see the expense or risk as something to consider or worry about. That made me worry. A lot.

The second and equally-vocal group were those who felt it was a colossal waste of time and expense. They felt the company was just fine and were of the mind that if it isn't broken, why fix it? I'm not sure this is true. Chris, our R&D manager, was the loudest in that camp and continued to question every decision we were making.

I knew that we needed to adapt and grow in this new digital age, especially if we were to compete in the industrial rental space. I could feel us falling further and further behind, and eventually, as Mark had so pointedly put it, we would become obsolete. While our numbers weren't reflecting it yet, they soon would.

The third group was the one that I subscribed to. In this group were those who felt that changes were needed but that we needed to do it in a thoughtful way and reduce risk where we could. Becoming a digital company was delving into waters that were not familiar, and Mark and his team were the experts.

We needed to adapt and grow in this new digital age, especially if we were to compete.

I liked the idea that we were the ones making the plan for our company with their guidance and assistance. I hoped that would create buy-in from the others.

"We hope you have taken the time to review our interviews and our suggested outcomes based on those meetings. We were very impressed by the respect your customers have for your company and their willingness to give valuable feedback that will position you to continue to work and grow with them in the future. That is a huge testament to the work you do," Mark said.

"My executive team and I have looked over and discussed your reports. We were very impressed, but I will have some questions for you as we review it today," I said.

"You are the experts in the industrial equipment rental space, and the stewards of your company. You obviously know what you are doing, and so we are not suggesting you stop everything that's working and try

something completely new," Mark continued. *"We want you to trust our recommendations based on our experiences with similar companies in similar markets. But at the end of the day, we want to work with your teams on your terms to create a plan that we will help facilitate for you."*

"That is such a relief to hear," I said. "There are those who are concerned about you taking over and not listening to them or, worse, that you are here to help us weed out and fire people."

"No, no. That's not our purpose at all. But you should be aware that, in our experience, about 80 percent of your staff will see this through and about 20 percent won't. That is not because we are suggesting firing anyone; it's because sometimes change is hard for people, and some will look for positions elsewhere."

"That isn't necessarily a bad thing," I commented.

"Not at all. As you begin changing to a digital culture, new positions will need to be filled. Of course, the first place we would suggest looking is internally. But some people don't want to do new work. This will open your company to fresh new talent and experts filling all-new positions, while some other positions will become obsolete. So, while personnel will change, it is a more organic process.

"You have a tremendous opportunity to not only help your business become a digital one, but there are also a number of new products and services that we believe you can begin offering, and huge potential from new AI technologies to augment—not replace—the value your people create. We are not going to tackle all the possibilities and capabilities in one session. We want to assess what your thoughts are and your capability to bring some of these new products and ideas to market."

"So where do we begin?"

"I'd like to talk about drivers, outcomes, and capabilities, as these will create the framework for selecting projects. Drivers are things that impact your business long-term. Do any of you have ideas surrounding this?"

"I think about things like marketing initiatives, customer loyalty, and company growth. One of my biggest drivers right now is that we should be top of mind for equipment rental solutions."

"Those are some great ideas. Becoming a digital company can help you with many of these drivers. I would add that the right drivers produce the right outcomes.

"Next are outcomes. These are the things that match up with your long-term and annual goals for the company. We have seen a list of your objectives this year. I'd like to add some outcomes based on our interviews with your customers."

Part of the process of ensuring the right outcomes is aligning your strategy to desired outcomes and vice versa.

Mark handed me a list, and while some of the outcomes were ones I could predict, others were surprising.

"I like the idea of more online service options. This is an area we had discussed but had little idea where to start. Even if we put order forms online for people to fill out, we needed people to manually add them to our orders and then send an email back. It didn't feel like a smooth set of operations, and because we needed so many people in between, it didn't exactly feel like self-service."

"I am glad you brought that up. What we would like to do is to take an idea like that and lean into it a bit to see what hasn't happened or why it might have failed in the past. Sometimes we think something is a bad idea because it didn't work the way we envisioned it would, but in reality, it could be other factors such as not enough resources being provided, or not providing exactly what customers wanted, and so we need to tweak it."

I was a little confused by his response. "Are you suggesting we spend time and resources on projects we know have already failed?"

"Not exactly. What I am suggesting is that we test something before completely dismissing it. Sometimes the solutions can be simple to bring an initiative to a place of success. And, you are correct, sometimes it is just a bad idea, but at least we can explore why it didn't work and then take what we learn to develop something else."

I knew that some of the teams would have issues with working on projects that had failed in the past, but I needed to be behind Mod Op Strategic Consulting's suggestions. I needed people like Chris to have an open mind or at least not be divisive.

"In order to accomplish these outcomes, you will need new capabilities. For example, in order to offer seamless self-service, you need to have the right people, processes, and technologies in place."

"So you are going to have us build a software platform? This has been something we have been struggling with. We have sunk a lot of money into it, with nothing to show for it."

"At this point in the process, we are just discussing options for your company. We have to be clear on what it is you need before we have a discussion of building anything. That is why we are meeting to begin the process of breaking down these bigger ideas into ones that you agree that you need; then we can begin to develop strategies around those. It could mean new software, but until we are clear on what problems that software would solve, beginning a project of that size could be premature."

That made sense, and it would definitely ease the minds of the board and our CFO.

"Many of these capabilities are going to be digital ones. Remember that technology is just a piece of the puzzle, not the whole thing. Right now, the majority of your orders come by phone. Your sales team takes down the information and creates a work order. While you do have software that

people can use to place an order, it is not very user-friendly, and it doesn't offer all the options your company offers. Even then, your sales team gets an order by email and then has to type up the order in another system. What is its major drawback?"

"It's slow, and we may be losing potential orders and new customers."

"Exactly. Right now, your salesperson writes up the invoice and sends it to the closest warehouse to the client to fulfill the order. Many of these orders are being faxed. In addition, if one of your salespeople leaves, all the documents and knowledge go with them. We suggest there can be more transparency in the process."

"Can you believe we still use fax machines?" I laughed.

"Exactly my point. But I don't want you to get stuck on the outdated technology—I want us to focus on what it represents."

"In addition to being an antiquated process, invoices often end up getting lost or misplaced."

"I visited one of your warehouses. The stacks of orders were over-whelming. There didn't seem to be a consistent system to fulfill them, and then when an order is fulfilled, it is shredded. Let me ask you a question: do you use a phone app to order pizza or other food delivery?"

"Sure."

"Have you noticed that when you open the app to place an order, it asks you if you want your same order?"

"Yeah. It's like it knows me."

"How many of your customers order the same equipment?"

I could see where he was going with this.

"I'd say most of our long-term customers order the same things. I think sales had a spreadsheet with their orders."

"Do your salespeople have that information available to them? Do the people at the warehouse?"

"I don't think so. But we have some amazing salespeople who can remember the customer and easily complete an order based on their previous ones."

"What happens if there is turnover? Remember, when a person goes, all of their knowledge of customers goes with them. Without a central repository of that information—that is easily accessible—that data isn't being used to its fullest potential."

"So are you saying we need to have a system that they can use to look up previous orders?"

"I'm suggesting maybe a bit more than that. Just follow me here for a minute. Once the order comes in, there doesn't seem to be prioritization. It doesn't matter how many pieces of equipment they need, the size of the order, or when the order came in. Some of the feedback from customers was about the length of time they have to wait for equipment to become available, or that when they expect equipment, it isn't delivered on time. When they call back to the sales department, they don't have any information on the progress of the order. If they are given the number for the warehouse, the phone rings and no one answers."

"They are telling me that they are too busy filling orders to answer the phone. They don't have time to deal with customers calling all the time for updates. I believe we can do better. If customers can't get answers and the process is slow, then they will find someone else next time that has a better process in place."

"I couldn't have said it better. Think about that pizza app. When you order food, it provides a time estimate for delivery. In some cases, you can even see a map where the delivery person is. Customers expect to know when equipment is being delivered so they can adjust other work being done on a site accordingly.

"Because systems are not connected, warehouses aren't sure if they will have a piece of equipment when a customer needs it. Because there is no

centralized system, they have to call around to see if other warehouses have a particular item. Then there is the process of getting that piece of equipment where it needs to be. This takes time and money. The greatest loss of money is in the form of lost customers. Because the system is slow and unpredictable, they are going to companies with a system in place that allows them to see their order and to see where the equipment is coming from and when it will arrive. You are already losing customers, and at the

> ## "The greatest loss of money is in the form of lost customers."

rate you are going, you could be down by a third or more of your repeat customer base in the next two years. Your acquisition of new customers is not enough to keep your business going. In fact, your new acquisition numbers are already slipping. Not to mention, when they place an order, wouldn't it be terrific if the online system could suggest upgrades or other related options? An intelligent AI-powered system could do that—in real time, customized to the client's needs."

These were all things I had discussed with my executive team, but we had never been able to create a cohesive plan for addressing the issues. We hadn't ever even documented the issues, let alone discussed them all at once. I quickly realized that these were the same issues that were keeping me up at night. We'd never spent the time required to create a cohesive plan for addressing these issues. I hoped working with Mod Op Strategic Consulting's team would be the solution we needed.

"Logistics is another area of concern. Consider that simple pizza app. A person logs in and hits a button, and their regular order is in the cart. They hit another button, and they pay with their saved credit card. Then they are presented with a screen that shows the progress of the pizza—from acceptance of their order to a map with a little pizza car moving on it.

When they are close, your phone dings and lets you know that they are approaching your house.

"I'm not suggesting that you create a phone app, at least not right now. But customers like to know where their equipment is and when it will arrive at their destination. They have many decisions, such as the starting time of a project. They don't want workers at a site with no equipment. They are paying for people to stand around, and that's bad business."

"Right now, if they call or email us, we can provide that information. We have a Contact Us page on our site."

"Yes, but do you always have the information available? And how long does it take to answer those inquiries?"

He had a point.

"Well, if they get an inquiry, the customer service rep can call the warehouse and ask …" I stopped, realizing what I was about to say. Customer service might call the warehouse, but no one answers.

"This is exactly where artificial intelligence can come in—not to replace your people, but to help them. What I want you to think about is how data is being handled and making it usable and accessible internally and externally. You have many systems containing redundant data, but they aren't connected. And some of the necessary data, like where a particular piece of equipment is, isn't accessible to the people who need it. This data is not only important for day-to-day operations, but you can also use that data to create new products and services, improve customer satisfaction, and generate stronger and more effective marketing campaigns."

"That sounds great. Will you be talking to the teams about this?"

"Absolutely. I'll have them imagine a customer coming to your website. They find the equipment they want, or they can access their past orders easily. They can choose the types of equipment they need for a particular job and enter their request for when and where they need that

equipment. They can do all of this without needing any live person to help them. If they have questions, they can use the AI-powered virtual assistant to answer most of them. They pay for their order, and an email is sent to them. The system processes the order and routes where the equipment needs to be and on what date. It doesn't need a human to do this. It places the order on a calendar and sets up the logistics. At the same time, the order is sent digitally to accounting. All of the information about the order and the customer is captured in a database that people who need that information can access. Marketing gets a notification, and the autoresponder sends them other offers similar to what they bought. The data from any additional sales is fed back into the system to make future marketing offers—for this customer and for others—smarter and smarter. Meanwhile, the order goes into a queue at the warehouse, so every day they know what is coming in and going out. The warehouses can see the inventory across the entire company. The delivery information is entered into the CRM, allowing the company to send communications on maintenance and replacement parts to the customer in the future. Finally, a short survey is sent to the customer to ask how their experience was."

I wanted to clap! That sounded fantastic. I couldn't wait for Mod Op Strategic Consulting to share that vision with the company. But then I thought of Chris and the questions he might bring up.

"People might be worried that we are going to scrap our current procedures, lay off a bunch of people, and have computers do all the work."

"Not at all. People, process, and technology are our focus. We still need people to run everything, and they will choose what projects to be involved in. This is about your vision, not ours. Each of the components of the digital transformation of the company will go through its own vetting and testing process. As we mentioned earlier, we are not suggesting massive changes all at once; however, we do feel that some of these changes

can occur quickly with little risk. We will need to prioritize your drivers and then your capabilities to determine things such as budgets and time needed to implement."

"I'm on board for anything you need me for."

"One of the questions we do have is whether you have a process of bringing a product from idea to launch."

"I don't know if we are exactly sure what you are asking," I commented.

"If you wanted to create a capability such as adding a more robust system connecting the data to all of the departments, do you have a process or strategy for taking that idea and walking it through to the point of having that system running throughout the company, ready to take orders, and allowing access to the data by key players?"

I was a little embarrassed to admit the truth. "I don't think there is a process in place like the one you are describing."

"We need to set up a day with Jasmine. She is our product development expert. She can help you create a plan so any new product or service you choose to produce will have a pathway to development. It will make things much easier and get new services and products to market faster."

"That sounds fantastic."

"And let me ask the same question about marketing. Do you have a process to feed information from marketing into the other departments, to better inform everything you do?"

"I'm afraid we don't."

"Then we should also set up a day with our colleagues at Mod Op to explain how they can add value on that end."

"That seems like it could really make a difference."

"Great, then let me get with your teams to have our initial meetings. They will be much like we have had today. After the introduction, we

will start to assess the feedback and our take on what we observed. Then the fun part comes as we brainstorm about what ideas have merit to investigate further."

"I can't wait!"

I felt very encouraged by the process and direction for the company. I felt less overwhelmed by the notion of becoming digital because we were developing a plan, one that everyone could be a part of.

***

WHAT DOES THIS MEAN FOR YOU?

It's important to prepare yourself and your staff to step in and to support and guide advisors as they continue to learn your business. Transformation is a collaborative effort, and your team will play a significant role in that.

As you do this, you should also know that change is not easy and that this might result in people leaving your organization. Help your employees by clearly communicating that change is on its way, and ask your partner for help in how to manage that change.

CHECKLIST

- **Business value scorecard**—Create your business value scorecard to help you weigh and prioritize upcoming work. Organize a meeting with your executive team focused on identifying key drivers, outcomes, and capabilities.

- **Take an active role**—Take an active role to help guide your partner through your business's nuances.

- **Communicate change**—Communicate change to your employees to help them adjust to new ways of working and/or new technologies.

- **Artificial intelligence**—Consider how AI can assist your staff, your customers, and your partners in solving their biggest challenges.

TOOL KIT

- **Business value scorecard**—This is a valuable tool to help you assess and prioritize (and eliminate) the work that is yet to come. The various dimensions of your scorecard allow you to assign weight to your business priorities.

LESSONS LEARNED

- Collaborate with your partners. Always work with your advisors to make plans. Leaders in their industry are the experts.

- Determine a few strategic drivers, outcomes, and capabilities that can help ensure a digital transformation is aimed in the right direction.

- Digital transformation is change management. People, culture, and processes are all at least as important as technology in any transformation.

- CEOs have to walk a fine line between leading and guiding their teams and also being aware that not everyone's mindset will allow them to make the journey.

RESOURCES

- https://dprism.com/insights/
  technology-budgeting-five-questions-ceos/

- https://dprism.com/insights/
  how-ceo-lead-product-strategy-execution/

CHAPTER 6

Implementing Modern Product and Project Management

The CEO meets with Jasmine, the product management expert at Mod Op Strategic Consulting, to discuss the strategies of managing digital products and services with a formal life-cycle management process. She discusses these processes and begins brainstorming ways the company can create their own process in order to be able to streamline the journey from product idea to managing the development of that product and then launching it. The company had no formal process, and so the CEO learns a lot from this conversation.

"Thank you for meeting with me," Jasmine said. "I spoke with Mark, and he brought me up to speed on where your company is in the process of developing products. He wanted to be sure we discussed what product management strategies were already in place and how to create a more formal system that can be used moving forward for any future product. We have a bit to cover, but I believe by the end of today's session, you will walk away with a better sense of what product management is and how having a more formal process, or at least a blueprint, will help you as you begin to develop new products for your company."

"My teams have been working on new software that would provide a portal for clients to use to order and reorder rentals," I said. "We started to internally develop it in house, but we ran into two issues. First, we didn't have people with the right skills to do coding, and the people we asked to work on it became overwhelmed trying to do the coding while still doing their regular jobs. So a year ago we hired a firm to help us."

"I heard that didn't go well."

"That's an understatement. It was an unmitigated disaster. After spending millions, we didn't have anything to show for it. The company we hired blamed us for not being clear enough about our expectations and that we kept adding new components, which made it impossible to complete it. The board wasn't happy, and thought I needed to talk to a recruiter about a new position somewhere else.

"It wasn't that I didn't agree with the company's assessment, but there was little communication happening during the development. We thought they had everything they needed, but I realize now they didn't. I already see the approach you are taking is helping us refine exactly what we need."

"I believe we can help you with all of that. My goal today is to take an idea and get a big-picture view of making it a product. Product man-

agement isn't the same as project management. Right now, my focus is on the product and how you develop it."

"Why is that important?"

"Like you pointed out, without a plan it will be hard to develop a product. I understand you don't have a team dedicated to product management right now."

"That's correct," I said, a little embarrassed. "It is one of those things we didn't know we needed until we needed it."

"Not a problem. That's why we are here to help. This is a common problem we see with a lot of companies—taking products from idea to reality. Creating a plan is part of the process, but equally important is a team with the right people to manage it."

"We do have excellent teams, and they come up with new ideas all the time."

Jasmine smiled. I was impressed by her demeanor and patience with me.

"So can you walk me through that process?"

"Our development team has meetings and decides what it is they want to develop. They then hand it to the appropriate department with a description of what needs to be developed and a timeline expectation."

> **"Creating a plan is part of the process, but equally important is a team with the right people to manage it."**

Even as the words left my mouth, I could see how short-sighted that might be and reasons that approach wasn't working.

"When we sent the client portal project to the IT team, they asked me for help all of the time. I realized only after a lot of wasted time and effort that the IT team didn't even know where to start. They were spending hours looking at tutorials on YouTube to try to figure it out. The feedback we received from the company we hired was about the specs. I wasn't involved in most of the meetings that were occurring, and I should have been. That is why we wanted to work with you guys. I had come to the conclusion that if we were not clear what we wanted the portal to do, why were we even trying to develop it?"

"That is an excellent point and a great place to start. You are understanding the why of product management. You can blow through a budget with a Waterfall approach and fail without a process in place and the right people in positions with the right capabilities.

"Let me ask: what type of prioritization framework do you use?"

"What do you mean?"

"When you have a number of projects to develop, how do you decide which comes first?"

"The teams usually handle them as they arrive."

"How has that worked?"

"Well, we have run into a lot of issues. Mostly I get reports of workers feeling overwhelmed, and then come the requests for overtime."

Jasmine wrote some notes.

"Again, these are not uncommon issues, and I would imagine that turnover also increases as the good employees have too much pressure put on them and the ones that are not used to increased output quit."

"Exactly!"

"It helps if you are clear and focused on what it is you're trying to accomplish. We call the list of projects a backlog. Developing a list that is prioritized will reduce that chaos. Every time a team finishes a task, your staff can look at the next item on the list and decide whether they have the people and resources to accomplish it. If they don't, they can either spend time gathering those resources or move to the next item on the list."

"I like that idea."

"*There are some questions you should begin to ask as you prioritize your list. How do you look at the return on investment? Are you doing this to innovate? Are you doing this to create the next generation of a product? Are there marketing implications? Can artificial intelligence add value? Then you can look at the documentation review from ideation all the way through to the actual development of that product and through the product launch. Product management is a process that repeats for each new product.*"

"So is there a decision-making process for prioritization?"

"*Yes, by looking at the actual product management team. Do the people on this team have the right skill sets? From what you have shared, you are trying to create a software product but don't have a software engineer on staff.*

"*Your product manager is different from your product owner. The manager is the one actually implementing the development of the product. He or she is working hand in hand with the developers to actually accomplish or create the product. This is different from the person who's actually coming up with the ideas. That's the product owner, the one actually building out the road map and thinking about the feature development and what's going to be required. So if you're building a customer portal, you would be thinking about a landing page, right? You would focus on what the customer does when initially logging in, and the development team would decide what that experience should be like. Once you come up with that idea, then you need to decide what it is going to look like and feel like. How do you want people to interact with that interface? How would you market it to users, new and old?*"

I knew some of the departments would be very excited to hear about this new approach.

"*Now we get to some of the things necessary to become a digital company. You will need to decide what kind of data you want to collect and what data you want to display to the customer. Once you have developed these things, then you can break these ideas into smaller pieces to create your backlog. This is where the prioritization begins because you may not be able to accomplish everything within that process. You may only be able to accomplish certain elements of that."*

Part of the process of ensuring the right outcomes is prioritizing according to your desired outcomes by creating a model to rank-order your ideas and work activities. Utilizing business value scorecards to align tasks to priorities is an effective way to progress when faced with competing priorities.

"Can you give an example?"

"You have to look at things like time to market and what features are the most important to the customer. You may not get the entire system in place, but you might want certain features to be available as soon as possible. Once those are accomplished, then you move on to the next item in the backlog. Looking at what is most important to the customer should weigh heavily in your prioritization because everything should come back to the customer. You need to make sure that you're building something that's intuitive yet also innovative."

"So what comes after that?"

"Once you have the right product to implement, then comes the governance piece to oversee the project. Governance is about standing up the project and creating a way in which the team is going to be interacting, leveraging the very same application they may be working on."

I could hear Chris's voice in my head about someone looking over his shoulder. He always wants to work independently, but that doesn't help the leadership of his team or how that team interacts with the rest of the organization. I was going to have to do some deep thinking about how Chris was going to fit into the new paradigm.

"Some of my people might say that it sounds like micromanagement."

"It isn't, because it is about understanding what a team is working on, not policing them. It is making sure they have what they need and are reporting back to the leaders and stakeholders about the progress of a project. Part of governance is about seeing where those dependencies lie, where you may need to jump in and assist. If there is some kind of block or challenge that a team is going through, you are able to figure out a solution."

"Mark mentioned your company provides this governance piece."

"Yes. Many companies such as yours don't have an internal governance structure. We not only provide the governance piece, but we also train your employees to take over that function."

"What else is involved in governance?" I asked.

"The person doing governance has metrics and measurements to look at from a budget perspective. They can report how a project is pacing and whether it is on budget and whether it will be completed on time. They are able to do this in real time because they work daily with the product teams. You know as the teams are rolling up their sleeves and jumping into some of these tools, you're going to face challenges, such as the way in which it's architected or something else they've forgotten about.

"We also do a daily scrum, which some refer to as a standup. This is a short daily meeting designed to let the team plan out its work for the day and identify any obstacles that could impact that work. Most teams hold these meetings in the morning and limit them to ten or fifteen minutes."

"So how often is the governance lead meeting with the teams?"

"We suggest having constant contact during daily and weekly scrums.

We recommend that team leaders come to this meeting to discuss what has been accomplished during the previous week. This is where dependencies can be identified."

"Dependencies?"

"If you are working on a particular application for your team and you need a database to capture data to be created first by another team, that is a dependency. Work on the application will be delayed, and they won't be able to accomplish their daily goal," explained Jasmine. "That is why a governance person is important. That person can help the teams work through dependencies and even avoid them by prioritizing the workflows in the correct order. The governance person will be able to predict the speed at which each team works. They do this by gathering data over time. They can more accurately predict when any given backlog item can be completed. In doing so they can mitigate dependency issues. They can also interface with marketing to figure out from the very beginning how to sell and promote this new offering."

"Obviously we have added new offerings over the years with minimal difficulty. This process is different in a digital company?"

"Traditionally, if someone has a new idea to build something, you take a hammer, some nails and wood, and build the thing. That approach doesn't work as well in the digital space. Because you are using data, a framework has to be built so that you have a structure to engineer around. It is a different process in which things are created in tandem and in order. Product management can assist you as you create a process that works for you. Once you have created that process, you will know where to plug in the different people, processes, and technology for each piece."

"So what is the next step?"

"We will look at your current projects and work with you to begin to prioritize them. Then we will break those down into smaller parts we call epics. In the case of the portal, we would identify the functions you want

and the infrastructure you need to build. Becoming digital all at once is not the goal, but you need to have an idea of what that looks like. You have received feedback from your customers and our recommendations. The epics are broken down into what we refer to as stories, and these make up your backlog. We will help you develop teams to tackle each of those stories. Mark will discuss more about that process, I am sure."

Even though I was getting some pushback from Chris and a couple of others that we could make the changes we needed internally, I knew this wasn't the case. We didn't have all of the infrastructure and processes Jasmine was mentioning. Watching a YouTube video on how to do it wasn't nearly enough.

"We are glad you are here to support us. More importantly, it eases my mind that you will be there to help us when everything goes off the rails, as I'm sure it will until we get the hang of it. Learning and changing is not a painless process."

"The good news is that the process I am giving you a quick overview of is done in phases. We are early in our work with you, still. You get to choose how involved we are in each stage. My goal for you today is to begin thinking about the process of product management, as this is important for every stage of product development."

"And we really appreciate your help with that."

"As we go through the stages, I will step in and help you with the product management and governance pieces. The focus is to save you money, not cost you more money. Failed products will cost you way more in the long run. I recently worked with a company that built video game apps. They wanted to add the voices of cartoon characters into the game. It wasn't a matter of whether they could build that feature; it was a matter of whether they should. They didn't want to invest in something that their customers didn't want. So instead of creating a bunch of characters, which is what was originally pitched, we chose one. They built it, and we

beta tested it. We received feedback directly from the customers and also analyzed data on how many times a user chose to use that feature. It was decided that it would not be a good investment to continue to add more character voices. If they had gone the approach of adding all of those voices and releasing them all at once, it most likely would not have gained them an acceptable ROI. In fact, some of the players of the game found the voice annoying and distracting. So not only would they not have recouped their investment, but they may also have lost loyal customers. You can absolutely pick and choose what you want us to do if that makes sense."

"It makes sense as to whatever services you suggest and can provide. It is obvious as I sit here listening that a better process of product management is needed. We are bleeding money on certain projects, and at the end of the day, we have nothing to show for that. I know there will be some questions from our finance people and the board."

"Like what?"

"Well, you are saying that you are evaluating projects as you go. You make changes as they need to happen and decide on ways to fix them. This could lead to cost overruns and an unpredictable budget."

"That is a valid concern. It can make budgeting a challenge. But at each meeting, we can assess how we are working within your budgets. We have discussions about whether to increase the budget to fix a challenge or if we need to take a different approach. As I said, governance and project management are not about micromanaging—they are about oversight. We never want you to get to the end of a big project and have nothing to show for it. Also, the more projects we do, the more data we have. We can create more accurate budgets based on past performance. This is where data can really help you. You don't have to make gut decisions; you can make them based on current data."

As we concluded our meeting, Chris came to mind. I knew I

needed to have a heart-to-heart with him about the future of the company. I hoped he would be on board and support what Mod Op Strategic Consulting was doing, but I wasn't sure based on his reactions up to that point. If he decided to leave, we would wish him the best. If he stayed, he would have to reduce his opposition and be a part of our digital transformation as a leader.

***

WHAT DOES THIS MEAN FOR YOU?

In order to bring your ideas to market quickly, and effectively incorporate the ideas of your customers, employ an agile process to build products.

You will have to assess your current organization's capabilities, play to your strengths, and bolster up where you are weak with partners and new hires. You will also have to begin to understand where artificial intelligence can fit in your organization and how it can help you achieve your goals.

An agile process coupled with an assessment will allow you to get a much clearer idea of the budget that you will require to deliver on your new and/or updated strategy.

CHECKLIST

- **Build a product process**—Build a product management process filling any gaps from your current capabilities. Include a feedback loop from your customers to integrate into the development process.

- **Get product management expertise**—Product managers are an essential component to making sure you are building the right product for your customers.

- **Be Agile**—Employ Agile development methodology to remain nimble through the development effort and accelerate time to market for priority features.

- **Align product to strategy**—Align your product efforts to your strategy.

- **Incorporate marketing**—Bring marketing in at the beginning of the process so you know exactly how you will sell and promote your new offerings.

TOOL KIT

- **Write user stories**—Take your customer feedback and turn it into statements of specific actions users need to achieve in order to get their jobs done. These will be taken by the development team and turned into the "technical requirements."

LESSONS LEARNED

- A product management capability or department is essential for developing new digital products. Product managers are the conduit between the needs of the customer and the developers who actually build and code the products.

- It is important to bring in or have the right level of expertise in product management.

- You can't do everything. A constant process of prioritization is critical to any digital transformation, and a CEO needs to ensure and empower the team to make these difficult decisions and trade-offs.

- Digital transformation is a full-time job for a significant number of people in an organization. Don't even start with a digital transformation unless you are prepared to put existing high performers into full-time digital transformation positions.

RESOURCES

- https://dprism.com/insights/accelerate-product-delivery/
- https://dprism.com/insights/technology-lifecycle-management-ceo-roadmap/
- https://dprism.com/insights/jobs-to-be-done-framework/

CHAPTER 7

Implementing Agile

"It's good to see you again," said Jasmine. "It occurred to me after our discussion about product management that perhaps we should talk about the best approach to these projects we have been discussing."

"It's great to see you again," I said.

"From our interviews with people in your company, we have determined that most of the time, when a new project comes up, you take what we would term a Waterfall approach. We would like to offer you a different, Agile approach, especially since we are helping you become digital."

Agile and Waterfall are two well-known project management methodologies. Both of them are popular in software development, but each is best suited for different types of projects. The main difference is that Waterfall is a linear system of working that requires the team to complete each project phase before moving on to the next one, while Agile encourages the team to work simultaneously on different phases of the project.

Samantha, who was our CFO, wasn't a fan of Agile, mostly because it was hard to create a solid budget around it. I hoped she would be open to the idea.

"We have found that each organization we have worked with comes up with its own version of Agile, one that works for them. This is based on the culture, the skills that you have, and how the CFO wants to view finance."

"I was about to say that Samantha, our CFO, isn't a huge fan of Agile."

"Don't worry; we will be working closely with her, providing support and answering whatever questions she might have. There are many external factors that determine what form of Agile you're actually going to implement. We want to work with you to come up with a customized version of Agile that meets your needs. We aren't going to give you a book that tells you how to do this. Instead, we are going to give you a set of principles and then help you figure out how to land those principles—which ones are more important to you than other ones. No matter what we come up with, it has to be sustainable."

"As I said, we tried an Agile approach before. It was a bit of a nightmare."

"Did you work with someone on how to best implement it?"

"No ... honestly, we read about it in a book." We both chuckled at that.

"I hope you will trust us. We are not going to meet with you a couple of times and then wish you luck. We are going to be with you every step of the way. This methodology isn't a one-and-done. It will take work and tweaks along the way. The great thing about Agile is that it is just that ... agile. It is flexible and adaptable. It is a methodology, not a template you have to follow. If something isn't working, you can make adjustments. The good news is you don't have to wait until a project is complete; you can make small adjustments along the way."

"We have had a number of cost overruns, as I mentioned about our last attempt at building a better customer portal. I'm concerned that with an Agile approach, budgets will be up in the air."

"I understand your concern, but you can make it a priority to keep it as a constant concern. In Agile, there is what is known as the iron triangle. You have three constraints to consider: time, dollars, and scope. You can prioritize two of those. You can't optimize for all three of them. When I say dollars, I mean resources. Things like the size of a team.

"For instance, you can optimize for dollars and time. Or you can optimize for time and scope, but then dollars will inevitably float. I understand the desire to nail down all three of those, but you can't. So you can prioritize money and resources, but you might need more time or need to change the scope. The flexibility of Agile allows you to do that."

"Okay, I'm following you."

"Consider a project you want by the end of the year. Now you have taken time off the table, so you are left to consider money or scope. To your point, money is often fixed in a budget, so you are left with changing the scope. That's the great thing about Agile. If you have a list of sprints you want to accomplish, which is what we refer to as a backlog, you can flex your scope in order to optimize time and money. Then you're just setting where in that backlog the floor is. You might only get through the first 250 items. But you will know this and work within that scope. We find it costs companies more in the long run to have a failed project using the Waterfall method, rather than flexing using Agile.

"The Agile approach is a process of continuous value delivery. The problem we have seen with the Waterfall approach is the failure to deliver value. Business leaders often have a vision of sitting in a room and spending four to six months creating a specification for the business. Once that is approved, the team assigned the project will go away for eighteen months with the hope of turning that specification into the software."

"That is exactly what we have done with the software we were trying to create before hiring Mod Op Strategic Consulting. It wasn't working, and we had nothing to show for our effort, except the loss of millions of dollars in promises that were never fulfilled."

> **"The Agile approach is a process of continuous value delivery."**

"The team comes back at the end of the eighteen months and says, 'Hey, we delivered what you asked us to deliver.' The business leaders spent six months developing the specification, and by the time the team began working on it, what they produced wasn't exactly what the business wanted. Because there was only a beginning and end to the effort, there wasn't any ability to change anything. This is what we see as the failure of the Waterfall method. This is why many organizations begin implementing Agile.

"These businesses get the overall philosophy of Agile and learn to create chunks to work on and sprints to deliver. They are able to be flexible and can make changes. The problem is that at the end of it, they don't actually deliver any value along the way. Perhaps they will deliver value eighteen months from now, or perhaps not. That is why we stress that the Agile approach is one of continuous value delivery. Without it, you experience all of the downsides of doing Agile, along with all the downsides of using a Waterfall approach. That's the worst of all possible worlds."

"I believe that is what we experienced when trying Agile before. We never made it to the end and opted for a Waterfall approach. We didn't see the value of Agile, I guess, because we weren't executing it very well."

"We see that a lot in companies we work with. That is why we are starting now to teach you the principles so that you do experience that value all the way through a project. As you will learn, we chunk up the

projects into what we call sprints. After two weeks, the team can dem-onstrate it to Samantha by showing her what they accomplished. It may not be a fully working piece, but it might be a smaller piece of a larger solution. It can be one feature that you delivered that your company can sign off on and everyone can see value in. Then you can move on to the next piece. You don't have to wait for months to see the completed project. It is an iterative process, like how a factory works. You are building a machine one piece at a time and repeating it."

"Is that where governance comes in? It sounds like a lot of moving parts that we will need help with, to keep it all moving smoothly."

"Absolutely. This oversight not only makes sure that the sprints are occurring but can help with issues as they arise, as well as prioritize what sprint comes next and which team will tackle that. The point we want you to understand is that in this process, you are creating and refining one piece at a time rather than trying to create everything at once."

"That's what I feel has happened to the software we were trying to create. We had this idea of everything we wanted to do and a budget and deadline when we needed to create it. We have been tripping over ourselves to try to get everything working all at once, and we have failed to get even one component completed."

"That's my point. You don't have to tackle the entire system. You can even create parts of it offline first. Try it out. You can choose to roll out a few new features at once and see how they do."

"That makes total sense."

"Remember when we talked about testing a hypothesis and seeing if it will be a part of your overall plan of transformation? Agile allows you to do this, whereas a Waterfall approach doesn't. So let's get into what this might look like for you.

"We like to decompose a product concept into epics, which are high-level themes of a project. Each of those epics gets decomposed into what

we call a story. And a story is a discrete deliverable. For example, if I, as a purchasing manager, want my client to be able to see the latest balance on their account every month, that's a story. That's a feature that can be coded. An epic is something like a self-service finance portal that has a set of features. Those features are the stories, and then that becomes your backlog."

"Is there going to be a quiz later? Do I need to take notes?"

"You can if you wish, but we have packets and more formal training on this that we will do with you and your teams over the next couple of weeks. Right now, I just wanted to give you a basic overview."

"Great!"

"Next, we break the work of those stories into sprints. Within those sprints, each team has a certain amount of capacity."

"How do we determine that capacity?"

"Great question. At the beginning of Agile projects, teams may set a goal of accomplishing one through twelve in the backlog. And then they start the sprint, do their work, and deliver. Problems may arise, but they get the job done. Instead of reaching their goal of twelve, they reach ten. They move the two that they didn't complete to the next sprint. Over time you can begin to get an idea of what a team's capacity is and assign the stories based upon their performance."

"You mentioned project planning and prioritization. Is that where this is done?"

"Exactly. Planning is where that backlog gets built. Planning is where you decide your product concept. Then you can decide on the epics and the themes. The team breaks down those themes into user stories. But you don't need to do all of that all at once. You can decide over the next three months, but at the beginning you are only working on epic 1. There may be six epics across the entire project, but you begin with just one for the next three months. You don't have to figure out all of the epics and stories

at the beginning. With Agile you do enough of a breakdown to understand what you need to build, and then you can develop a backlog. As you progress, you keep filling that backlog while at the same time figuring out how much capacity the team possesses and how much velocity they have."

"What if your team doesn't have enough capacity?"

"You scale Agile by adding more teams. Agile teams are typically small, around four to six people, and they each have their own backlog. The teams might have six epics they are working through, and you might decide that you can only afford three development teams. That is how you can keep better controls on the budget using Agile."

"Our finance people will like hearing that!"

"Now you have three teams working on their own epics—1, 2, and 3. Each of them works through their backlogs while having a parallel process going on. But now, there is a new challenge, and that is running into dependencies. In this scenario, you may be working on the fifth story in a sprint, but you have to stop because team 2 has to deliver their second story before you can move forward. The more teams you have, the more important dependency management is. The person handling dependency management has to look at these possible dependencies and move stories around to prevent them from happening while realizing the impact that these changes may have on the schedule.

"As I mentioned before, the benefit of Agile is regular reporting to you and your leadership team. You can drill down to the individual team level or individual sprint level. Consider this: you are looking at the performance of your customer service team. You could look at the macro level and determine if the project is on track. If not, then you would want to drill down and see where the problem is. There is so much you can learn from doing a retrospective at the end of each sprint. You can identify and fix problems in preparation for future sprints. That's the iterative continuous improvement part of the process."

We exchanged some final thoughts and set up some future meeting dates.

"This will be an ongoing process and learning experience. So if you have questions about any of it, we are here to answer them. This will provide the framework moving forward, so it is essential you understand Agile."

I waited another hour to have a meeting with Chris. We were going to discuss how things were progressing. I had received reports that he was still not being cooperative with Mod Op Strategic Consulting and gave them a hard time when they tried to teach him and his team some of the new processes.

Another hour passed, and it was obvious he wasn't coming. I went directly to Chris's office. I opened his door without knocking. He sat there looking shocked and had his phone to his ear.

"I'll have to call you back," he said and ended his call.

"Why weren't you at the meeting?" I asked pointedly.

"What meeting?"

I didn't know whether he was being serious or playing coy. In either case, I didn't have the patience.

"You know what meeting," I said as I closed the door behind me. "We were supposed to have a follow-up discussion about how you were getting along with the Mod Op Strategic Consulting team. I understand that you haven't been meeting with them like you were supposed to."

"I'm sorry, I got busy this afternoon. I didn't really see a need for us to meet. I haven't had too many interactions with Mark or Jasmine. They tried to explain Agile to my team, and I told them I had other things that needed my attention. We tried Agile before, and it didn't work, so I felt like my work was more of a priority."

I took a couple of breaths and thought about what I was about to say next.

"I made it clear that working with the consultants was your number-one priority. You were given specific instructions and were given a warning that your attitude toward Mod Op Strategic Consulting and the work they are trying to implement wasn't acceptable. Not showing up to meetings with Mod Op Strategic Consulting or me because you didn't think it was worth your time is a clear message to me and the rest of the people at the company."

Chris leaned back in his chair with his hands behind his head.

"And what is that? That I believe this is not the best use of resources? That they are talking about stuff we have already tried? We are behind on the software development, and that has to be my priority."

"The message is that you don't fit in the current direction of this company," I said.

"What are you saying?" replied Chris with his eyes wide open.

"It means that at the end of the day, I will need you to clear out your desk. Consider this your termination."

I turned toward the door.

"Wait … wait," he said in an indignant voice. "I'm too valuable to this company and have seniority here. You can't just fire me."

"It's a shame, Chris, that it has come to this. You have been a valuable part of the company. I don't mind giving you a good recommendation. I just don't see you coming with us on this journey any further."

"You can't do this," he said with his arms crossed.

"You're wrong. I just did."

***

WHAT DOES THIS MEAN FOR YOU?

It's important to remember that not everything has to be perfect before you embark on your transformation journey. Your strategy, team, and objectives absolutely should be carefully considered, but much of your plan should be flexible in order to give you wiggle room to adjust your course as you learn new things without throwing away your budget.

Agile does just that. It is more than a "methodology." It is a set of principles that can be adapted to your company's needs and provide you with value early and often as small chunks of work are tested, delivered, and iterated on.

CHECKLIST

- **Adopt Agile**—Learn about Agile's principles and its benefits.
- **Employ a scrum master**—Find the right talent to help you implement, teach, and lead Agile at your organization.

TOOL KIT

- **Agile Manifesto**—Leverage the Agile Manifesto to learn about the twelve principles of Agile.

LESSONS LEARNED

- Perfecting a Waterfall plan may help calm your nerves in the short run, but you might end up with nothing to show if it's not exactly what the business wanted. Agile can help solve that by delivering value immediately.

- Adjusting how you view your capitalization and operational expenses is an important part of planning for a transformation project.

- Not everyone is suited for the journey you are about to embark on, and some decisions will be difficult ones.

RESOURCES

- https://dprism.com/insights/
  organizational-ambidexterity-product-innovation/

CHAPTER 8

Program Management and Implementation

Mark and I settled into our seats across from one another at the conference table. This was a weekly ritual that I was becoming used to and also looked forward to.

"Do you think we are ready?" I asked.

Mark settled into his chair and opened his laptop.

"How do you mean?" he asked.

"I'm still nervous about how all this will work. I have my CFO and the board breathing down my neck. Everyone is concerned about the budget and what to expect."

"I know this is a bit different than what you might have been used to in the past. Looking over your past projects, you have taken more of the Waterfall approach. We set the goal, and off you go."

"Yes, but look at the mess we are in now with the customer portal. We have spent over a million dollars and have nothing to show for it."

"*That is why we feel an Agile approach will work much better. You will know how the project is progressing in real time. You will see progress and applications on a regular basis instead of sitting on your hands. Marketing will be plugged in from the start instead of reacting to a finished product at the end, unsure how to excite customers about it.*"

"I hope so. I just don't know what to expect or my role in all this."

"*First, take a deep breath. You brought us in to make things easier, not harder. Sure, there will be an adjustment over the next few weeks as everyone gets used to this new Agile approach, but we have your back. I will be involved in the process daily. I will help those implementing the work and those managing it, and most importantly,* I will be helping you understand the data as it comes to you. You will be able to alleviate the stress of the board and your CFO because you will be able to show them progress in a way that you haven't been able to in the past.*"

> **"This is a fluid process … We will make changes regularly and pivot when needed."**

"Is there a manual you will use or something I can begin reading? Even though I don't have much extra time, if there was a cheat sheet, at least I could be ahead of the curve and have something to refer to."

"*As I mentioned, this is a flexible process, not a one-size-fits-all. We are customizing the process for your company. So, I'm sorry, there is no definitive book I can recommend. This is a fluid process. As we work through the projects, we will make changes regularly and pivot when needed. It is hard to predict when those might happen or what they will look like. What is important is that we have discipline around project and portfolio management.*"

"Tell me more about that."

"It is important that everyone is working and integrated throughout the company. We recently worked with a company that didn't have a cohesive system in place. It was a bit of a mess."

"What happened?"

"They were working through projects and sending updates regularly about their progress and challenges. The problem was that they weren't updating each other between the projects, and each team was doing things differently. In addition, because they didn't have an agreed-upon system and analytics, the way project leaders were reporting was different between divisions. They were reporting in different ways that did not connect with each other, and they were all looking at the data differently. They were reporting apples to oranges rather than apples to apples. This made it hard to know how projects were progressing or how the portfolio as a whole was doing. For instance, if I call something a defect and you call it a bug, we may be talking about the same thing, but we aren't using the same language. So, at the top, it was hard to determine what needed to be fixed or if the things being reported were the same issue."

"So what did you do about it?"

"This is what I mean about having a common discipline. In that company's case, we had to reorganize the tools they were using to report into one system that they were all using and also ensure that they were using the same terminology. We brought in a new portfolio management tool for them to use. This helped us elevate all the granularity in the day-to-day operations into something within which they could actually report the overall program pacing."

"Will we have to do that here?"

"The good news is that we are starting the projects with portfolio management tools to begin with so we don't run into those sorts of problems. It is what we have been working on with your teams to customize the tool so that it makes sense and is easy for anyone using the system to understand. We

have also incorporated artificial intelligence to review the reports and help make sure the data matches and everyone is using the same terminology."

"So a bug is a bug, no matter who is talking about it?"

"Exactly! Your CFO will really like this because she can see that projects are on time and within budget in real time. There will be fewer surprises, and she can make better decisions regarding changes. She won't feel she just has to keep throwing money at a project hoping that will make it work better or faster."

Program-level dashboards are essential at indicating overall progress and health to board members, executives, and project teams. The dashboard uses key project metrics and helps establish a common language.

Timeliness

- Planned hours versus actual hours
- Spikes or unanticipated work
- Time to completion (a.k.a. burndown)
- Scope creep

Budget

- Budget/cost

Quality

- User satisfaction
- Number of bugs

"Which is where we have been this past year. We heard there were overruns and overtime, which meant more money, but there was nothing to show for it in the end."

"This kind of discipline helps eliminate that. You will be able to see if a particular data piece is falling behind. That can have implications for other dependent parts of the project. This kind of data will help everyone."

"It sounds like a lot of transparency is built in."

"Absolutely. You can look at any part of the project and determine where the issues are. Usually, these issues fall under people, process, or technology. You can determine quickly what will fix the problem and get that project moving again to prevent traffic jams later on."

"Can you walk me through some of these disciplines you are putting in place?"

"Sure. One of the areas we are putting into place is a meeting cadence. We have daily standups."

"I think Jasmine talked about those. Can you remind me what those are?"

"The teams meet and discuss what they are working on that day. They talk about what they worked on the day before. Whether or not they accomplished what they set out to do doesn't matter. It is a good time to talk about any roadblocks they may have. These standups happen worldwide at the beginning of the day. Since you are a global company and have global teams, this is important. If you have part of a team in Europe meeting with the North American team, they are halfway through their day already. They must address their issues immediately so they are not delayed. By the time they have the global meeting, they will have already resolved those issues or will be ready to address them with the rest of the team."

"There have been times when our European teams have complained they haven't been able to get any work done because of the time zone issues and they are sitting on their hands."

"The more quickly issues are addressed, the less downtime there will be. Your teams were having weekly meetings, which is fine, but it is not enough

to address issues when they arise. These meetings help keep projects moving. As a backlog item is completed, there is a discussion of what is next, who will be assigned to it, and what roadblocks need to be addressed."

I liked the thought of moving projects along, and having my finger on the pulse of what was going on was also a plus.

"Can you explain the process again for getting our customer portal online? And then how the Mod Op process helps us get there?"

"I'd be glad to. From the beginning of a project, a product owner will be selected by you. They will work hand in hand with the program manager. They will determine the most critical features that must be delivered at a particular time. In your case, it will be a year to roll out your new customer portal. They then decide what items need to be completed; these are broken down further into backlog items. The reporting is a continual process of how those items are progressing. The program manager helps keep things on track and makes changes when needed. They oversee everything and report how things are going back to you, your executive team, and the board.

"In addition to the daily standups, we will have biweekly sessions and go through and refine things as we see progress and identify issues. I know this differs from how you have done projects in the past."

"Yes, which is why I am trying to wrap my brain around all of this. I'm sorry if I am being a slow learner."

"Don't apologize. I am glad you're asking questions. Whatever we can do to help you understand and support the process will help us and those working on these projects. In these biweekly meetings, we can demonstrate new features. You won't have to wait until the end to see the complete rollout. This is an opportunity to make changes in the middle of the process rather than making costly changes at the end."

"In the company I mentioned, the CEO and the CFO didn't know what had been completed and the project's progress. The product sponsor *was dealing with the day-to-day work but wasn't using the tools already in place to report what was happening and the fact that the project was in trouble. When it came time to reveal the final product, no working model was shown. They spent millions of dollars fixing the project because they had to scrap what they had already been working on in the last year—or, more accurately, not working on."*

I felt a lump in my throat because that was precisely the position we had been in when we hired Mark and his company to help us become more digital. I had lacked the vision that becoming digital meant that we would be retooling our process and how we did just about everything. While the enormity of the shift was overwhelming, I felt we were on the right track.

"Is that something we will be able to do?"

"Absolutely. You will be able to clearly see where progress is slowing down. You will know what questions to ask and where to direct those questions. You won't have to wait for the biweekly meeting; you will be able to access up-to-date data at any time."

"That will be amazing!"

I could walk into meetings well informed. It would be nice not to have any surprises. I would know what was going on and be ready with any questions from the board.

"It seems the transparency of this process will quickly identify if there are problems with a particular team or even with someone working on that team."

"Once the tool is in place, there won't be any fudging of reports to make the team look good or give the illusion that everything is on track when it isn't. That is what the governance piece is. They are the gatekeepers to ensure the data is accurate and up to date. They will have a ground-level view of what is going on and be in the best position to make recommendations—hiring someone, moving someone off a project, and more.

"*We have found it is better to have a third party monitor progress. They are neutral to the data. They make sure that reports are accurate and have no other motive than to ensure the data is clean. The CFO loved the process because they could see the deliveries and knew more accurately the budget and how long a project would take.*"

"My CFO will love that."

"*Like I said, we will have daily standups and meetings with the leadership teams every two weeks. We can identify risks and create plans for mitigating those risks. We will also set up a monthly meeting with the highest levels of leadership. This will look at the project's progress and allow you and your leadership team to ask questions and determine what else can be done to ensure the projects are moving forward.*"

> I couldn't expect buy-in at the production level unless I had buy-in from the leadership team first.

I wrote down some notes as he continued to talk. This was a new way of doing things, and I wanted to be sure that the leadership team was prepared and that I was in support of the new process. I couldn't expect buy-in at the production level unless I had buy-in from the leadership team first.

"*We have found that this process builds confidence within an organization. This approach allows the leaders to pivot quickly because they are aware of what is happening more often and more clearly. As the projects are completed and we start to roll out, you can have the assurance that the foundations we lay will continue. We don't want you to be dependent on us; we want to make these processes familiar and ingrained in your company.*"

"It sounds like there will be a lot of data coming in, and it seems a little overwhelming for me to have to sift through that every day."

"I can totally understand that, so we will be simplifying the system using red, yellow, and green in reference to the projects. Red denotes those things have stopped because of a dependency, the need for other resources, and things of that nature. Green means that things are running on time and on spec. Yellow means they may be a little behind on their production and need help. You will also be able to see the progress of a particular project as a percentage. The tool we are using crunches all of that information, and makes it easily interpretable using AI tools, so you can use it in your meetings."

"Since these are new processes and new tools, how will we learn all of this? It seems that there would need to be a lot of training before we could succeed."

"We will be teaching through guidance and experience. We are bringing in some of our project managers who are familiar with the Agile process. They will help bring you and your project managers up to speed and simultaneously get the ball rolling on some of these projects."

"So they will learn on the fly?"

"In a way, but our people are very good at teaching and guiding with the goal of rolling out the process and then handing the reins back to your people. In addition, I will be meeting with your leaders to get updates on how they are progressing on the milestones and what we need to keep things moving forward. I will bring that information to the weekly and monthly meetings and then bring the solutions to the teams about how to mitigate any challenges they may have."

"So what happens if we determine that a project needs more resources, whether an increased budget or even more personnel?"

"The beauty of the Agile approach is that you will know that as the project proceeds rather than at the end. You will be able to respond to those challenges more quickly. In addition, there is a continual process of planning and assessment. With discipline in place, it won't feel like the building is

in flames when an issue arises. We will have people in place to walk you through. Because this is a transparent process, you won't have to worry about too many surprises. Sure, there will be things that you can't anticipate when you start a project that you will need. Still, at least there will be a pathway to fixing things efficiently and without being in a panic."

The idea of the CFO not coming to my office with that look on her face that said she was about to deliver some rather unpleasant news would be refreshing, to say the least.

"How soon will we see results from the system you are putting in place?"

"As soon as we have the right people in place and have identified the projects we will be tackling first, you will see value delivered quickly, even within those first few weeks."

"Will you choose those projects, or will we have input?"

"As you know from the beginning, we have collaborated with you, and the rollout and execution will be no different. That is why we want you to have the most accurate data possible to decide the direction of the projects and the resources being used."

"That is a question my CFO continues to ask me. How will the money be used, and what is the spending pace?"

"Because this is an Agile approach, you will see the progress of projects and have a much clearer idea of the progress and the amount of time they take to complete. It is much different from waiting until the end of the project and being told more money is needed, even though there is nothing to show for the money that has already been spent."

"Not only will the CFO be glad to hear that but the board as well. How much time will the teams be expected to devote to these projects? We have been working on this customer portal for a year, and now we are saying they will have to do it all over again. I don't want to fatigue them."

"We will bring in help, and also in those daily and biweekly meetings we will be able to check in with the teams to see if they are feeling overwhelmed and overburdened. You will have a sense of whether to slow down the pace or to allocate more resources."

"The guys in R&D and IT will be delighted to hear that. Marketing will be excited to have early deliverables to look at as well. It has been a tough sell, as you know, to get you all in here and help us overhaul the company's operations and procedures. We must be able to show value to the executive team and the board as quickly and consistently as possible."

"Your success is our success. We are committed to helping you achieve your goals. In this system, there is a huge accountability piece. Because there is transparency, we will know where the issues are and hold the owners of those pieces accountable. That includes what we are doing. If we are not helping your teams to produce value, then we aren't doing what we promised you that we would do."

Mark made a good point; every time I talked with him and his team, my trust and confidence in them grew. They were genuine and smart, two things we had lacked working with other consulting companies in the past.

"When do you project that we will be able to get the teams rolling?"

"We are three-quarters of the way through, so I would say another couple of weeks. If it's okay, let's continue to set up these meetings so I can update you and help support you in getting your teams to shift their mindsets. It won't happen all at once, but your commitment will go a long way toward inspiring others around you."

"I'm all in. I trust you all and feel things are going in the right direction. Now I need to transfer my confidence to the board."

***

WHAT DOES THIS MEAN FOR YOU?

To ensure success, it is up to the executive team to remove as many obstacles as possible and ensure that progress is tracked in line with the shared vision. Coupled with an Agile approach, project health will be easier to assess in order to reprioritize work as needed.

CHECKLIST

- **Track progress**—Identify and track key business and program metrics to ensure that you are staying on track.

- **Scrum "ceremonies"**—Set up all of your scrum meeting needs to ensure consistent lightweight checkpoints on progress, achievements, upcoming work, and blockers.

TOOL KIT

- **Reporting**—Use available tools to build a reporting dashboard to enable bottom-up reporting on project progress.

LESSONS LEARNED

- It is essential that an organization adopts a common set of analytics or measurements for tracking each project; otherwise, it can become confusing and difficult to compare progress, issues, etc.

- Daily scrums, or standups, allow the team to discuss issues and accomplishments from the previous day, plans for the current day, and any potential roadblocks so that they can be addressed in real time.

- An Agile project approach allows you to see the progress of projects and have a much clearer idea of the progress and the amount of time they take to complete, avoiding painful surprises at the end (common in Waterfall-approach projects).

RESOURCES

- https://dprism.com/insights/a-checklist-for-successful-transformations/
- https://dprism.com/insights/accelerate-product-delivery/
- https://dprism.com/insights/definitive-guide-digital-product-strategy-management/

CHAPTER 9

Managing Change

"Mark, thank you so much for meeting me on such short notice," I began.

"Not a problem at all. In your message, you said there were some issues with pushback from a couple of your employees?"

"Yes. Some of it I've been able to divert to department heads, but every day I hear about more complaints, especially during morning standups."

"What sorts of issues?"

"People feel things are changing too fast and can't understand why we are doing it. They report that they liked the older, simpler way of doing things and don't understand why they needed to do things differently. My concern is that if it continues, it could begin to affect the morale of other people, including my department heads, as they feel the pressure."

"First, I'm glad you came to us with this because we can definitely help you. Second, you can take a deep breath. This is totally normal. Change can

be hard for people, and sometimes despite our best efforts, the people we are trying to lead remain opposed to the new ways of doing things."

"That's a relief because I felt like I had a mutiny on my hands."

"The ability to manage change is paramount to the success of any transformation within an organization. The good news is that you are embracing the change, continuing to support your people, and holding firm to the vision of digital transformation. Effective change management will drive commitment across your organization and ignite partnerships and shared commitment to that change among your executives, your leadership team, and all of your employees. It's the key to the success of your implementation."

"We have just begun some of the implementations, and it feels like not everyone is on board yet."

"One of the things that will help is partnering with you to create a change management plan. We have already built part of that plan through transparency and open communication throughout your organization. Because of that, you are hearing the complaints and feedback of your employees."

"That is very true. In the past, if issues arose, they were a real mess before I heard anything about it, but now I am getting daily reports, and that has been a game changer. I can head off potential issues and create solutions quicker and more effectively. How can I help them through these changes?"

> Change management is a key part of your transformation journey and is equal parts creating a climate for change, communicating change, and training for change. The various change models that exist help manage both personal and organizational change. With the right plan in place, you will be able to manage and enable alignment with overall goals and vision.

"Consider this analogy for a minute. Imagine you're a student joining a class for the first time. After entering the room, you find a seat that will likely remain your seat for the entire duration of the term. If someone were to sit there, it would spark a feeling of uneasiness and disruption to your routine. Why? Because no one prepared you for this change, you need to navigate the adjustment with no guidance or support. Just when you thought you were getting yourself situated with the new class change, your routine was again disrupted by the change to a new seat."

"Okay. I can visualize that."

"I know this is a simplistic example, but this is what happens with change management. Change affects people in different ways. Now think about your company's digital transformation. No matter the size, a business transformation needs and deserves the same preparation and thought as all of the key decisions it took to get there. Regardless of the positive gains on the other side, it introduces a wide variety of emotions and feelings from all parties.

"Change management ensures that a transformation is managed not just from a technical perspective but that it also focuses on the people. You are saying that you are getting feedback that some employees are unhappy with the changes. Without employees feeling empowered, informed, trained, and committed, a transformation will lose steam and ultimately cause damage to the business."

"So how do we build that change management plan?"

"The strategy has several moving parts. As we progress through the projects and are consistent, successful change management builds and maintains momentum. It will be best if you continue to engage and include your stakeholders whenever new changes are being considered. Be sure to take the time to train and develop your people. Your employees can become frustrated if they are given several new tasks with no training on how to do them. Change management continues even after your initial

goals are met, and a good strategy ensures your company's readiness to face new challenges while at the same time creating stabilization."

"I've heard several employees ask about new technology. They wonder when they will get new technology and toys to work with. How do I get them to understand this might not happen for a while, as we aren't sure what we need?"

"Well, you have already started by having daily scrums. You must reinforce the idea that digital transformation is not just about technology. This takes getting them to shift their mindset and focus on the changes needed for a true digital transformation."

"They are also asking about AI and how that will change things."

"Again, AI is a tool, nothing more. There is plenty that we can get from modern artificial intelligence tools, but they come into play after we figure out strategy and priorities, not beforehand. Don't worry—again, it's a mindset shift. Transformation isn't about the technology; it's about the kind of thinking that takes place."

"That seems like a difficult task."

"I'm not sure that it is so difficult, as we feel it is more about strategy. When we first met with you and your executive team, we established the case for change. We helped you establish a change management strategy and the means to monitor and communicate throughout the process. So the infrastructure of change management has been laid. You may need to review these points with your management teams.

"Remember that clear communication with your stakeholders, executive team, and management teams helps move people into action by getting the right message to the right people at the right time."

"I like that. I'm writing that one down!"

"Communication is different for each team you are talking to—for example, the messaging for your technical teams will be different than the messaging with your executive team. You must define your communication

principles, as that will drive all your communications no matter who you are engaging with."

"How do I communicate the need for the changes we are implementing so that they become more engaged in the process?"

"You need to identify how the employees will be impacted by change. You need to be able to speak their language and understand what is important to them. This takes listening as much as it is about speaking to them.

"Before you communicate with them, outline your key messages and plans. Be ready to address their concerns, and be proactive in your approach. Remember to tell them that you want their feedback and reiterate how important that is in the success of the projects they are involved in. Just like you use your marketing team to communicate with customers and prospects, you need to also use marketing internally to communicate what is going on. And just like we can help with the external marketing, we can also use our expertise to help with internal marketing as well.

"These changes are a learning process. Ensure you provide the right level of guidance up front and continue those lines of communication throughout the project. And, as I have said, change management isn't a one-and-done conversation. You are trying to get your employees to adopt a long-term acceptance of change and understand how it benefits everyone in the organization."

"It sounds like a lot of work for me to do. How will I be able to do this on my own?"

"The great news is that you don't have to do it alone. You will want to identify and develop change agents throughout your company. A digital transformation is about changing roles, processes, and working methods. In addition to having a well-thought-out change management strategy and plan, you need to identify the right people to help you execute it.

"Your strategy will outline the curriculum needed, any required material development, the training delivery schedule, and a plan for employee evaluation.

"Think job aids, tutorial videos, and FAQs—tools that can be shared across the organization and serve as a reference point for embracing the change and answering questions the end user might have. Often, key program team members who become subject matter experts in their areas of work, known as change agents, will run the training sessions. However, this does not happen effectively without the right level of planning—and that starts with the strategy.

"Equipping the change agents with the right level of detail and involvement in the feedback loop, and highlighting the value of well-documented information, will prove to bring a steady level of awareness and continue to empower the change to grow organically."

"The best change agents are the ones who believe in the goal and use their voice to drive adoption."

"You mentioned that change management is about readiness and stabilization over time. Can you explain this a little further?"

"I'd be glad to. Reaching the right level of readiness and stabilization does not happen without the proper sequence of change management activities.

"Prior to launch, all prior change activities will enable the entire program team to be inspired to be a part of the transformation, declare their commitment, and understand how they can contribute to its success on behalf of the rollout.

"While most roles in a transformation are assigned based on function and skill set, the best change agents are the ones who believe in the goal

and use their voice to drive adoption. Ask for volunteers to become ambassadors of the change!"

"Yes! I believe that might help those people who are not quite on board with the changes happening."

"I want you to understand that what you are experiencing is perfectly normal. Do you know the 80/20 rule in business?"

"Yeah."

"Well, in this case, approximately 80 percent of your organization will be resistant to change and may need to be urged out or moved to less critical roles. Conversely, approximately 20 percent of your organization will embrace the change. Identifying and empowering those people can help your organization move to the next level. This doesn't mean you have to fire 80 percent of your team. A lot of this change will happen naturally. People will step up, and others will see that their skills are no longer valuable in this process and begin to look elsewhere for new opportunities, whether within your organization or outside of it. The great news is that the 20 percent who embrace the change will become the champions and can bring some of the 80 percent along with them. Even if someone starts out skeptical, it doesn't mean they will end up skeptical in the end. Some of our clients' biggest successes have been built on people who were initially part of that 80 percent but learned that there is so much potential in moving to a more modern way of thinking."

"I've been hesitant to make any personnel changes as we have been onboarding this process, but I understand that some people will need to shift around or leave the organization. On the upside, it provides opportunities for those who are fully engaged to move to new, more critical positions."

"Exactly! Once you have identified your key stakeholders and change agents, be sure that they are committed to driving change with each launch of a new project and beyond. The change agents ensure that their employees

are satisfied with the level of support they receive, and they adopt changes. As people become more used to the changes, the transition through change in the future will become smoother, and you will have less resistance. Change in the future will be less of a shock and will be embraced based on past success."

"That's good to hear."

"As you develop your plan for change management, you should consider encouraging innovation. Part of the approach we are helping you implement is the ability to fast-track new ideas and test them in the marketplace quickly and inexpensively. Also, because we are increasing communication at all levels of your organization, people will become more comfortable sharing their ideas. In addition, we have been working on creating a feedback loop with your customers so that they may provide you with even more ideas for future products."

"Yes, we have already been receiving some of that feedback."

"That is why change management is so important. Project managers can add new ideas as time is available for your teams to develop and test."

"This all sounds great, but I have to be honest. I'm still nervous about this change process and how it impacts the company."

"We totally understand, but remember, we are in it with you and are available to help you as challenges arise."

"That is a relief, and we appreciate all you are doing for us."

***

WHAT DOES THIS MEAN FOR YOU?

It is easy to think about digital change as technology, products, processes, etc., but the people component of change is actually the most critical and often not given the necessary attention.

Therefore, a stakeholder engagement plan is essential—employees need to feel empowered, informed, trained, and committed to keep the initiative from stalling.

Digitally empowered cultures have several key attributes that allow them to successfully navigate change: customer centricity, innovation, collaboration, transparency, and decentralization.

CHECKLIST

- **Clear communication**—Establish the case for change early in the process, with a clear communication strategy that identifies the audiences impacted, determines appropriate channels, outlines key themes and messages, and establishes a clear communication cadence.

- **Highlight change**—Change management needs to focus on the impact to people as much as the impact of technology, process, etc. People want to know how their jobs will change, if they will be able to learn new skills, etc. Transparency and communication can go a long way in ensuring buy-in.

- **Assess your talent**—Assess your staff on their ability and interest in change, reward and upskill the ones who have potential, and ensure that the resistant ones are not in a position to derail the process.

- **Internal marketing**—Treat these internal initiatives as having just as much need for marketing resources as external messaging to clients and prospects. You need to sell this to your team, so use the talent you have on staff and the help of expert outsiders to do so as effectively as possible.

TOOL KIT

- **Change management plan**—Create a change management plan that includes communication that highlights changes, the impact of these changes, timelines for change, and how to get help.

- **New job descriptions**—Assess capability gaps and hire to fill those gaps as you go through your transformation.

LESSONS LEARNED

- The 80/20 rule applies to change management—approximately 80 percent of an organization will be resistant to change and may need to be urged out or moved to less critical roles. Conversely, approximately 20 percent of an organization will embrace the change, and identifying and empowering those people can help your organization move to the next level.

- Leadership needs to be flexible and adaptive, as the strongest digital talent is in high demand and will often seek organizations where they feel a strong connection and the ability to make a difference.

- Innovation needs to be encouraged. This can happen in many ways, ensuring that innovative approaches are encouraged (with budget, attention, etc.). Setting aside money for R&D can help accomplish this.

RESOURCES

- https://dprism.com/insights/
  navigating-change-management-and-digital-transformation/
- https://dprism.com/insights/
  digital-culture-how-to-instill-grow-and-measure-it/
- https://dprism.com/insights/
  embracing-change-ways-to-improve-agility/
- https://hbr.org/2019/03/
  digital-transformation-is-not-about-technology
- https://dprism.com/insights/to-beat-your-business-goliaths-
  let-a-feedback-loop-be-your-slingshot/
- https://dprism.com/insights/accelerate-product-delivery/

CHAPTER 10

Educating the Board about Digital

"How are things going?" Mark asked.

"Overall, I believe we are making progress. I see daily reports and feel more confident talking to my team leaders."

"That sounds fantastic!"

"It is, but now I need to meet with the board. It's been six months since I proposed working with you, and while they are seeing progress, I need to report to them about the next steps and what they can expect in the next year. I don't think we are done working with you yet."

"We will work with you as long as you need us to. Our goal is to give you all the tools you need and also to train people to fill in the spaces we are now occupying in your organization. As you know, just hitting your current goals is only the beginning."

"So do you have some recommendations for getting the board to share the vision of continuing to grow as a digital company?"

"I do. The first thing you need to do is to be able to tell a story. What will your organization be like three or five years from now?"

Mark passed some papers across the table.

"This is what we refer to as a future retrospective. Imagine it's five years into the future, and you are reporting the things you accomplished that year to the board. You've changed your relationships with your customers because of our new portal. As you describe this future retrospective to your board, you are creating a story, a vision of what the future might look like. It gives an idea of what your successes will be rather than saying you are thinking about doing those things."

> **"Just hitting your current goals is only the beginning."**

"I get it."

"So that is the first thing—tell a story and consider making it a future retrospective. The next thing to be clear about is that a transformation differs from a single project. Projects are part of a transformation. You are very early in that transformation, and as you finish those projects, you continue to further that transformation. As we have been saying, it isn't just about the next portals or ways of handling invoices. It is bigger. You are transforming the entire organization. Transformation changes an organization's DNA, how it operates, and what it can do versus a project establishing just one thing."

The simplest and most effective way to explain to your board why you are investing in a transformational project is to use a future retrospective to communicate future capabilities and vision. Let your third-party partners explain the governance and methodology.

"Tell me more about that."

"*Transformation is usually about capabilities. For instance, what are your digital capabilities? What are your sales capabilities? What are your marketing capabilities? What are your communication capabilities? You know what I mean?*"

"Yes."

"*It is about how they apply those capabilities to the transformed organization. So those are the first two pieces—(1) what's the story and (2) it's not a project; it's a transformation. The third part concerns ROI. Having met your board, I can confidently say they want to hear about ROI. They want to know about upside on the growth of revenue or savings or expenses. The ROI can be tough to project, so keep it straightforward and conservative. Don't overpromise and then underdeliver.*"

"Got it."

"*Then it is up to you to create that future and keep the digital transformation moving. You continue the transformation the same way we began: by truly understanding the voice of the customer and creating a capability around it. We met with your customers, interviewed them, and shared what we learned. It would help if you continue to do that process regularly so that your transformation is in accordance with the needs and wants of your customers. At this stage, you can be creative. You can have new customers, new categories of customers, new markets, and more.*"

"That sounds exciting."

"*It is. Consider market intelligence, innovation, and specific product and service strategy and how you can build it. And don't forget to translate what you learn into your marketing initiatives—which is something else we at Mod Op can help with. That's the story you want to share with the board. Keep the vision strong in their minds and show them your progress and new future retrospectives. We suggest sharing this information with your board to update them on your projects and how the company trans-*

formation is progressing. You can hold yourselves accountable for a list of milestones you have established with us and, once we are gone, with your senior leaders."

"It makes me nervous when you say you will be gone."

"We are still a phone call away and will follow up with you. If things go off track, we can be there to help set you right again."

"That's a relief."

"So, getting back to the milestones. You will return to them in six months, twelve months, and eighteen months. You will report your progress on those milestones. Those milestones drive the projects you are working on. We have already helped you establish your initial milestones, but you will revisit them and decide what your new milestones are on a regular schedule. This will help your board become comfortable with what you are doing and feel they are in the loop."

"Yes, a few of the board members constantly want updates on everything."

"We have helped you establish a method in which you will know daily the progress of your projects, but you don't want to watch a pot of water boil. Progress can be seen over time rather than in small increments. That is why I am suggesting having a regular meeting that they can count on, dedicated to your progress with your milestones. It sounds like those board members are nervous that they don't know what is going on or that once they learn of something going awry, it would be too late and cost the company a lot of money."

"There is a lot of truth to that. Remember I told you when you started working with us that we had spent a lot of money on a new customer portal, and by the end of the year, we were out over a million dollars and had nothing to show for it?"

"Yes, and that's why it is a good idea to set up the expectation of a regular accounting of your progress and projections of whether you will

achieve a particular milestone. Then you can decide if further resources are needed or if different people are needed on the project, or perhaps you might need to scrap it and consider a new milestone."

"That makes total sense. I have to say, I already feel more confident, as I can see how our current projects are going in real time. It helps me sleep better at night, and our CFO feels the same way as well."

"That's great to hear. As you may already realize, sometimes you're going to hit those milestones square and center, and sometimes you may miss a few things. You will learn from the misses and adjust things as needed. You'll keep your original plan as the core measurement, and we can tell you where you need to shift things. We are training people to do this as we go. Projects are often complex, and so changes are expected."

"The other thing I wanted to talk to you about was our employees. We have had a handful leave the company, but you said to expect this. We don't want to lose more if we can help it."

"Change management can be difficult. We are really focusing on capabilities so that they are prepared and ready for those changes. This is a big part of the digital transformation you are undergoing.

"There was a big shift when we went from an industrial workforce to a knowledge workforce and then to a service workforce. This shift to a digital workforce is no different. The capabilities and the skills needed will continue to shift, and people will need to be retrained for those positions. There is also the power of artificial intelligence to consider. Some people will find elements of their jobs replaced by AI, but the good news is that frees them up to do the more strategic, ultimately more important work that only humans are able to do. I know we've just started our implementations, but I am sure you have already seen that artificial intelligence tools can make things easier for your customers as well as produce new opportunities to handle data and information internally. With a well-

trained AI system, help for your employees is literally a click away 24/7."

"I have already noticed a big shift in the service industry. Automation and AI are everywhere you go. Fewer people are needed to provide services, for example, in grocery stores and restaurants."

"Except those people are still around. They're just doing more important things. Yes, some workers may need to be retrained in new jobs. Sometimes that means that they will need to be trained by companies if they aren't coming in with those capabilities. But we will find ways to unlock the value of as many people as possible and put them in roles where they can add even more value. We have been assessing people and positions and have begun helping to develop training programs."

"Yeah, I heard you were doing that."

"This training and shifting are important. I have seen many businesses close their doors because they lack the personnel or ability to retrain people to new positions. In their attempt to become a digital business, they find themselves painted into a corner. The service industries suffer as many people shift to other positions, sometimes at home. In some places, it can take forever to get an Uber. And some of my favorite places to eat have been closing."

"Yeah, I've noticed that myself."

"I want to ask your thoughts on allowing people to work remotely from home."

"To be honest, it makes me nervous. Do you think it is a good idea?"

"I can tell you that many companies are allowing more and more of their employees to work from home some days or even work fully remotely. We have seen it reduce business costs, as less space is needed. The employees are happier, as they can be flexible and avoid commuting to the office. Overall, we have seen that companies allowing remote workers have seen a greater increase in productivity."

"Are you sure? That's what I'm worried about—I'm not sure they are doing their jobs if they are at home."

"The structure we have set up for your company allows you to clearly see employees' productivity. Through technology, they can still meet with team members and team leaders. They are still accountable for making progress on the tasks assigned to them. Part of your reporting to the board will be about your projections for your workforce. You will need more employees for some jobs and fewer employees for others.

"For instance, you will need fewer accounts payable clerks or general accounting clerks because AI and new systems will auto-process that stuff. You will need more engineers. It won't be necessary to hire them, as you will more than likely subcontract out that work. But you will need to have people who really understand how to leverage the digital platforms and interact with customers. You will need to know what positions will be required as you grow digitally, which is an ongoing process.

"Not too many years ago, nobody considered the power and importance of having a presence on social media, but now it is a regular practice. So you will need social media experts—marketing—to train your customer service team to work with customers through the various gateways. Marketing will need to have specific capabilities across a number of different social media portals. All of these will require specific skills."

"I've heard people in marketing worried about being replaced by AI tools that can write copy better and more on target. I know AI can take into account trending keywords and calculate the best places to advertise and what copy will work the best."

"That is all true—to a point—and we will help you navigate all of it. But remember that AI isn't infallible, and still needs human input and assistance. These are learning machines, so sometimes what they produce can be clunky and, dare I say … robotic. There is a new position now needed in companies—AI editors. These people can read and edit AI

copy to make it sound more human. So your people, even those doing the same things that AI can do, too, won't necessarily lose their jobs. Instead, they may shift what they do and need new skills. What AI isn't good at is being creative. AI can simulate what other people have produced, but they can't develop totally new concepts and ideas. We still need humans involved, especially well-trained ones like our team at Mod Op—who can help with all of this."

"This is all great information and gives me a lot to think about before our next board meeting. I am very optimistic and excited about the future. I just hope that the board is as excited."

"Your enthusiasm will be contagious, so don't worry."

***

WHAT DOES THIS MEAN FOR YOU?

Transformation is not a project; rather, it is a much larger program made up of many projects. The progress of that program should be communicated to the board without losing sight of the vision and future capabilities that it will afford the organization. To communicate the vision and the transformation's raison d'être, use a future retrospective.

With an anchoring to the vision and capabilities in place, use KPIs to tell the story of how you are getting there in order to clearly communicate progress to your board.

CHECKLIST

- **Board governance**—Redefine board governance needs for your company.

- **Communicate vision and capabilities**—Use a future retrospective to communicate the vision of what's to come.

- **Share milestones**—Report on progress and overall project performance with KPIs that track you to important capability milestones.

- **Engage third parties**—Engage a third-party facilitator.

- **Governance**—Connect risk, compliance, audit, and ESG for stronger governance.

- **Artificial intelligence**—Understand what AI can and can't do, and deploy it in ways that amplify your company's power.

TOOL KIT

- **Future retrospective**—Use a future retrospective to communicate vision and capabilities to your board. Highlight what the future looks like and the capabilities that you will gain from embarking on a transformation project.

- **KPIs**—Identify important KPIs that track toward your transformation milestones.

LESSONS LEARNED

- A third-party facilitator can help the board understand the issues and the governance of a digital enterprise.

- There are digital tools designed for board governance. Use them!

- The board expects the CEO and C-suite to guide them through this change.

RESOURCES

- https://www.thecorporategovernanceinstitute.com/insights/
  guides/a-board-members-guide-to-digital-transformation/
- https://www.diligent.com/insights/
  governance-in-the-digital-age/

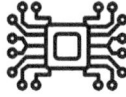

CONCLUSION

Congratulations! If you've gotten this far, there's no doubt you're ready to take the next steps. We hope reading this book has helped you envision what digital transformation could mean for your business, and, if we've done our job right, you should be asking the question, "How can I get started?"

The truth is, the way you can get started is exactly how we start the journey for most of our clients: first, with thorough market research to understand the landscape; who your customers are and what they need; who is meeting those needs right now and how; and where your own current capabilities stand, both in terms of data/technology and people. How well positioned are you to move toward the future?

From there, we architect a plan. How can we innovate to get you from here to there? What capabilities do you need? Who needs to be trained, and in what? What needs to be built, from an infrastructure point of view? How do processes need to change? What does the ideal future state look like, and what's the best road map to achieve it?

Once you have that plan, the next question is how to operationalize it. We have calls all the time with executives who are trying to do just that, and the honest truth is that there are two options. You have smart people; you wouldn't have gotten to where you are without them. They can almost surely figure all of this out. It will be hard, and it will take time and money, and mistakes might happen—but you can get a third of the way there, halfway there, or maybe even all the way there on your own.

You can also ask for help, from people who've done this and who do it every day. It's not an admission of failure to do so. Far from it.

We don't presume to be experts in your business until we come in and talk to you and your team and really understand who you are and what you need. We de-risk the proposition of change because we've seen it all before and know where the pitfalls are.

It is often more expensive and a far lengthier process to try to shift your business in a digital direction solely with internal resources. And it takes your team away from the day-to-day business activities that matter to your customers.

A firm like ours can bring order to the process and the technical expertise needed—but also the ability to change culture and convince your staff why the digital vision is so important. Without a team that fully buys into change, you face resistance at every turn. On the other hand, when every member of the organization understands how important the transition to a new model is for current and future growth, you unleash creativity and allow everyone to shine.

There's no doubt that navigating change is hard. Simply as humans, we often struggle to embrace change, and sometimes despite our best efforts, the people we're trying to lead remain opposed to new ways of doing things. In a business environment, transformation can become disastrous if done wrong.

As you can see from this book, becoming digital is about far more than technology. Sooner than you think, you can be on the road to the ability to compete better—now and in the future, no matter how your industry or the broader economy evolves. If you'd like to talk about how we can help, we'd be delighted to start that conversation.

Thank you so much for reading this book, and we hope it gave you a new and valuable perspective on the transformation to becoming a digital organization. Good luck!

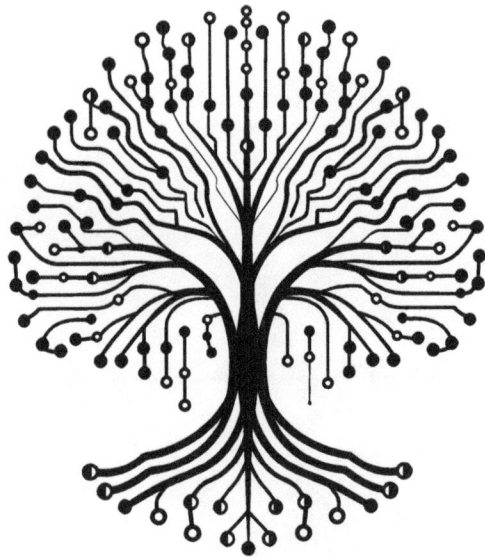

ACKNOWLEDGMENTS

Mod Op Strategic Consulting (originally known as Digital Prism Advisors) was launched by Adriaan Bouten in 2014 with a simple premise—that digital transformation was an incredible opportunity but also a threat for many organizations. Now, ten years, more than fifty clients, and hundreds of engagements later, the premise that our team could use its deep operating experience to help clients thrive has proven accurate.

We'd like to thank our clients for taking a chance on a digital consultancy that was initially short on consulting experience but well versed in the actual strategic and operational challenges of "getting digital done." Now, ten years later, we are proud to say that we have both the business experience and the consulting experience to make the process as seamless and easy as possible for our clients.

In addition to our clients, we would also like to thank our employees for choosing to work with us and making Mod Op Strategic Consulting an organization we are incredibly proud of.

This book itself would not have been possible without the professionals at Advantage Media and our colleagues at Mod Op, including our CEO, Eric Bertrand, and key members of our team, past and present, including Alex Abboud, Krissie Axon, Jennifer Cardella, and Matt Tosiello.

www.ingramcontent.com/pod-product-compliance
Lightning Source LLC
Chambersburg PA
CBHW031406180326
41458CB00043B/6630/J